GOVERNANCE
for
A NEW ERA

Robert Stephen Higgins

Note: This book was originally published in January, 2020 under the title Government for a New Age. This edition has some minor modifications of content for the new title and for consistency of the text with the title. Also, minor editorial improvements.

Published by Bradich Books,
160 Macdonell St., Unit 901, Guelph, Ontario,
Canada N1H0A9
http://www.bradichbooks.com

Data for Cataloguing in Publication
Higgins, Robert Stephen, 1941 -
Governance for a New Era/ by Robert Stephen Higgins
Includes bibliographic references.

1. Political Science. 2. History & Theory
   JC585.H54 2020 323 C2008-906007-5

Dedication

Dedicated to my beloved children Darrin, Andrea, Brian and Carlene and my always supportive wife Ivanka. All put up with me lost in thought on many occasions and hopefully this book is justification and redemption.

Contents

Introduction

When it comes to government it is easy to see ourselves as leaves in a stream, a disposition that effectively gives away our power because we can actually think and analyze, we can talk and write, and we can vote. If we do not pay attention to what governments are doing we may not detect disastrously wrong direction until it is too late. The bad consequences will affect not only ourselves but also our children - possibly more so - and our grandchildren. If we want a government that we set up and then let to do then it must be a proper government and one we can trust to perform adequately and honestly.

The following pages will use the term "proper government" in a particular way. It will mean a government founded on valid principles that, like science, are always true everywhere and the government puts the interests of the electorate first. Importantly, it will also mean a government that is not a tyranny of any kind, whether dictatorial, ideological, religious or indeed any optional philosophy to which some people fully subscribe but not all. Rather, the government will protect the individual person and allow the maximum practical amount of individual freedom. The theoretical development is discursive, like mathematics, discovering starting principles that cannot be denied and building on them to make a complete theory. In so doing it brings order to political science and lifts it to a true science from its present status as a quasi-science that simply describes present and past forms of government. The development is presented in chapter 3 and is the core of the book.

That development begins with a clean sheet of paper in regard to the design of government. It is preceded by a description of typical democratic governments, which may bore the reader already familiar with them, but it is helpful to first describe the vehicle being worked on to comprehend why its replacement is prudent. More so, it is vital to point out the important forces bearing on governments so that the playing field is understood.

CHAPTER 1

Modern Democracies: A Synopsis

Structure

A central feature of a democracy is a legislative body that consists of members elected by the people on a one person - one vote basis. The legislature may include one chamber - unicameral - or two independent chambers - bicameral. A unicameral legislature is sufficient when only the interests of the total population need to be considered and a bicameral one is believed necessary where the interests of groups of people united by some common factor such as regional identity need to be considered. A bicameral legislature may also be set up to provide a second look at intended legislation by an independent body. The United States of America is an example of the former where the House of Representatives consists of members elected from constituencies composed of sub-divisions of the population by area and the senate consists of members elected from each state (equal numbers per state). Canada is an example of the latter with a senate that loosely represents regions of the country but more so is considered a second view of bills passed in the primary house (House of Commons). The unicameral legislature will be considered the default form here but a particular country may opt for a bicameral one for one of the reasons above.

The legislature studies - usually by committees appointed for the purpose - and then debates bills that are proposed to the house. If passed they become law when signed by the head of the government. In parliamentary systems the head of the government is usually called a prime minister but some countries have other titles, for example "Chancellor" in Germany. The head of the country, i.e., head of state, is a different person such as a monarch (UK, Netherlands and Sweden) or President (France and Germany). In congressional systems the head of the government and the head of state are the same person, for example, in the United States of America.

The Party System

Another feature of almost all democracies is the party system of politics. Almost every democracy exemplifies, in its own way, this element of politics. Styles and substance may differ, but each party will put forward representative candidates for election and bear the cost of promotional campaigns which, in a big jurisdiction such as a province or country, are much more than all but the very rich can afford. The object is to win a seat in the legislature so that the elected person- a party member- will vote in favour of the party's program. If the member refuses then he/she is promptly ejected from the party and must continue his/her mandate as an independent member of the assembly without support of the party, particularly in the next election. The reason for this discipline has to do with the party's reason for existence which is to put in place by legislation its long term objectives for the province/country. It is also because the party made certain promises to the electorate during the campaign and must fulfill most to maintain credibility. Without political parties it is difficult (but not impossible) to find a mechanism for establishing and following long term goals because members of the legislature, ministers and the head of government are elected for the relatively short term of four or five years. Such a short horizon is not conducive to making long term plans or taking responsibility for solving long standing problems. The intractability of such problems as homelessness, illicit drugs and illegal immigration are examples.

Political parties arise when a group of people recognize common beliefs in how the country should be regulated and these people unite into a political party. In the simplest case the parties differ in their choice of which values come first and the range of things to value politically are similar country to country. Accordingly, the most common parties in the world are the following.

Conservative- The name comes from the emphasis on maintaining mainstream human life according to family, tradition and established institutions. Conservatives respect their history and antecedents and are not easily swayed by trends or fashions. Gradual change is preferred over sudden disruptions. Because conservatives prefer less government regulation of business and smaller government generally, they have been accused of favouring big business interests over those of the common worker. Possibly aggravating that impression is the attitude that the individual person is financially responsible for obtaining his/her needs.

Responsible financial management ranks high on the list of values on the premise that spending must be within revenues, much the same as the stable household operates. They will borrow for particular projects, much as a business or family would.

Socialist- socialist parties focus on solving the problems of poverty, deprivation and the concentration of wealth and believe the capitalist system is to blame. Their solution is to involve the government in the management of industry. Their approach after World War II was to nationalize key industries (takeover ownership with compensation to the owners). This proved unworkable in a changing economic environment, e.g. the switch from coal to oil, and was reversed in the 1980's. Since then the socialist approach has been to legislate businesses and persuade corporate executives to include regard for workers and families in their distribution of profits but if necessary to confiscate businesses to achieve a satisfactory amount of wealth equalization.

Liberal- a social and political philosophy that has evolved since its inception two centuries ago. Its first intention was to wrest power from ruling elites and by the turn of the twentieth century that goal was accomplished. Attention was then turned to emancipating the individual person from all constraints on his/her freedom, at least as much as practical. The constraints included firstly, disregard for individual rights by governments and employers and in society at large, but as the century developed so did the identification of poverty, disease, discrimination and ignorance as constraints on freedom. Because poverty was blamed on the poor distribution of wealth, liberals adopted socialist programs to rectify the problem and worked through government to remove the other constraints on freedom. In this century liberalism has arrived at a comprehensive ideology that addresses all the workings of society and the economy.

Libertarian- unlike any other party they believe that the primary purpose of government is to protect people's rights. The huge apparatus of government is superfluous to this purpose and should be dismantled. They believe that people will achieve better results by spending their own money than paying high taxes that has the government spending the money instead. Consequently, libertarians advocate small government, and less welfare state. People are required to take more responsibility for themselves and their needs.

Single issue parties- such parties try to obtain seats in a legislature so they can promote a single concern in deliberations. These could be the interests of a particular tribe, religious group, the protection of the environment or a language group, to name a common few.

Almost all ideas that result in new laws come from the philosophies of the above classes of parties. If one party has a majority of seats in the legislature its policy platform will dominate, which can result in some bills being passed that do not conform to the majority will of the population. This happens when the majority party has the support of only a minority of the population, a common result in first-past-the-post (FPTP) type elections. This way of conducting elections is used in nearly one-third of democracies and has its peculiar attributes. The main one is the difficulty for new parties to get a foothold in the legislature and the gravitation toward a two-party system. In the United States, for example, the Democrats and Republicans have faced off in both houses of the legislature for 160 years. Generally, third or fourth parties can elect members when they profess an ideology or possibly a religion that has a large following or when most party followers live in the same geographic area. The United Kingdom is an example where the Scottish National Party resides essentially in Scotland.

When no party gains a majority of seats an alliance between two or more parties must be formed to achieve a combined majority of seats. This results in a compromise of political platforms which many say makes for better government. Such alliances (coalitions) are common in those countries that have proportional representation (PR) of parties in the legislature. This means that a party that achieves X% of the vote will be granted X% of the seats, approximately, and has the benefit that a variety of policy objectives will be given a hearing and may influence legislation. PR does not preclude, however, common ideological themes from influencing legislation. Western Europe, where social democracy prevails, is such a place. The ideological current will be discussed later.

The debate over method of voting is about which method is most successful in representing the preferences of the people. As worthwhile as this endeavour appears it is transcended by the propensity of political parties to push their agenda regardless of what the people want. This tendency is more pronounced in the twenty-first century but in reaction a number of populist parties have arisen in Europe. They were formed by people fed up with governments making decisions that apparently went against the preferences of a large proportion of the population, sometimes the majority.

Financial Management

For the wide range of services provided by government, from security to infrastructure maintenance and much in between, it is understandable that it spends a large proportion of the money spent in a country. As the services have increased greatly in breadth since the mid-twentieth century the money spent by government has increased correspondingly. In Austria, Belgium, Denmark, Finland, France, Greece, Hungary and Italy government spending exceeds half of the nation's Gross Domestic Product (GDP) and the other democracies are not far behind (OECD Data, 2017). At the other end of the money flow is a voracious hunger for money. This is particularly true of national governments because of their responsibility for defense and other national programs. The money is raised mainly by a taxation system that is comprehensive, substantial and relentless. The government claims a proportion of every wage earner's income stream and the proportion increases according to the wage level. The calculation is not done on a "quid pro quo" basis but is intended to get the money from those who have it. The tax formulas are set to take as much as possible before measurable damage to people's incentive to work or striving for promotion to a higher position. The following hypothetical situation illustrates such a problem.

In Denmark, in 2017, the marginal rate of tax by all jurisdictions on a worker's pay was 55.8% (data by OECD Stat). If a worker was offered a promotion with a 5,000 euro pay increase (per year) then he/she will receive 2210 euros in after-tax income. The "value added tax" would consume 25% of that on purchases over 200 krone (27 euros), or 550 euros, leaving the worker with 1660 euros of actual buying power which is about one-third of the wage increase. This does not account for extra taxes on particular consumer goods such as tobacco products, alcohol products or fuels, nor for indirect effects such as disqualification for student aid loans for his/her children. With governments taking two-thirds of the wage increase while making no contribution to the promotion, only a person who has more interest in the prestige or who does not do the above calculation would try for such a promotion. Some governments saw this effect of high taxes and moved to lower them. An example is Canada where the marginal tax rate reached 54.6% by the end of the last century (in Ontario) and subsequent governments lowered taxes.

When the revenue from taxes is insufficient to pay all outlays governments will borrow money and this has turned out to be a recurring feature of the welfare state. As its installment proceeded in the 1970's the debt of governments, particularly national governments, began to rise rapidly. The following bar chart shows this increase quite clearly in 12 advanced countries (in this case advanced in debt).

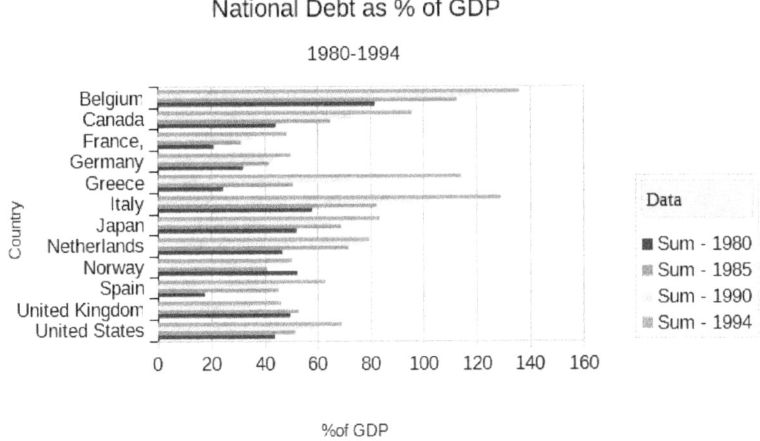

- International Monetary Fund (IMF) data from 1996

By the mid-1990's it became clear, even to the most socialist countries, that the trend could not continue. Some countries bit the bullet and returned to balanced budgets by the end of the century, e.g., Belgium, Canada, Germany and Netherlands.

The need to borrow money increased dramatically in 2008 in the wake of the financial crisis that threatened an economic depression unless governments borrowed money to support the financial system and stimulate the economy. The debts resumed their upward climb. The following table shows the debt levels in 2017 for countries that had become welfare states.

National Debt as a Percentage of GDP in 2017

Belgium	128	Australia	68
Canada	114	Austria	102
France	123	Denmark	53
Germany	76	Finland	75
Greece	188	Hungary	97
Italy	156	Ireland	84
Netherlands	77	Japan	235
Poland	72	Sweden	60
Portugal	146	United Kingdom	119
Spain	117	United States	127

- Data from Organization of Economic Cooperation and Development

Election expenses, on the other hand, are not a substantial expense for governments because they pay only the cost of the election apparatus while the heavy expense of election campaigns is paid by the political parties that put the candidates in the running (except for a few independent ones). To obtain this money the parties undertake a visible and solicitous campaign of fund raising. At the same time cost is reduced by a heavy reliance on volunteers. The expenditure of money and energy in an election campaign is impressive, especially when wealthy interests inject much money into campaigns such as in the United States.

Some governments economize by not paying employees well but instead providing serious job security. Indeed, in many countries, a job with the government is regarded as a job for life. However, with no penalty for bad performance and for wasting government resources the reputation of government for inefficiency has become firm in the public mind.

Influences on Government

With political parties having a great hunger for money to pay for election campaigns and moneyed interests wanting something from the government it is not surprising that they come together in the activity of donating to political parties. Donors fall into one of four categories: individual, companies, labour unions and public funding (from the government). In 2018, in the USA, donations under US$200., which presumably came from individuals, comprised about 30% of total donations. In the United Kingdom, in 2018, donations came from the following categories as a percent of the total.

Individual- 33.8%,	Trade unions- 16.9%,
Companies- 21.8%,	Public funding- 27.5%

Individuals and trade unions put their money where their hopes were. Companies placed bets or made investments on which they expected a return. The public funding was an attempt by government to reduce the influence on government of people who have money. It also gave small parties a chance to obtain a seat in Parliament.

In the late twentieth century a new purpose of corporate contributions arose with the objective of government support for globalization which made practical the operation of big business internationally. It gave companies the opportunity to sell products anywhere in the world (more or less) without the burden of tariffs and also the freedom to locate factories in the cheapest country for labour and sell in the country having the highest prices, again without tariffs. The effects on the economies of individual countries were considered to be purely incidental but the effect on permanent jobs and high paying jobs was profound, not minor. What ensued was the stagnation of the average wage and the greater concentration of wealth in the hands of people who had the money to invest in profitable enterprises.

The reaction to this trend has been a growing yearning for a European style social democracy that would require consideration of workers in the decisions of the capitalists. Sympathetic billionaires, as well as labour unions and grassroots organizations have been putting money into political parties to help bring about this conversion. The left wing parties are now well funded.

Another kind of influence on governments is the presence of lobbies, usually located in the capital of the jurisdiction where they maintain offices containing many professional (paid) lobbyists. They represent unofficial constituencies and their purpose is to construe pending legislation to favour those constituencies. In the United States the following are the top ten lobbying industries in terms of money spent (according to OpenSecrets.org for 2016).

Pharmaceuticals/Health Products	$63,168,503
Insurance	$38,280,437
Electric Utilities	$33,551,556
Business Associations	$32,065,206
Oil & Gas	$31,453,590
Electronics Mfg & Equipment	$28,489,437
Securities & Investment	$25,425,076
Hospitals/Nursing Homes	$23,609,607
Air Transport	$22,459,204
Health Professionals	$22,175,579

There are other advocacy groups that have other purposes, for example, watchdog groups that rate the actions or expressions of politicians, corporate leaders and heads of organizations, or the safety of products including food and drugs. There are groups that promote preservation of the natural environment, even generating "green" political parties. These and others try to influence governments to follow their priorities.

Another substantial influence on national governments is their relationship to each other, particularly in regard to regular trade, military and political alliances. The matter of trade affects the economic well-being of the subject country which causes it to defer to its partners' wants when practical to do so. Alliances can include formal agreements on military cooperation, for example. As no man is an island, no country is an island in relation to other countries if it wants to be involved in the business of the world, whether commercial or political.

Most countries have endorsed certain international treaties which are usually binding, putting onto the national government constraints which can have a substantial effect on the country, both financially and socially. These range from required spending on military forces to accommodating migrants who walk into the country claiming refugee status. The latter phenomenon has been having a pronounced effect on Europe in this century as other cultures are increasingly making their presence felt.

International Business Arrangements

International business arrangements are a major driving force behind government action. They usually involve trading some government prerogatives for concessions on trade, banking, industrial standards or protection of the environment. A brief look at each of these will help to understand constraints on government.

Trade

All democracies trade with other countries for at least four reasons:

- to obtain needed raw materials or manufactured goods or services involving a great deal of know-how and which are scarcely available at home.

- to obtain manufactured goods because the manufacturer has moved his factory to another country (per globalization).

- to obtain food products grown in better climates or soils or water availability.

- to sell goods and services to another country, thereby expanding the market and revenues and offsetting the cost of imported things.

To achieve satisfactory trade agreements government will probably have to compromise on trade terms. This is especially true if the country has joined the World Trade Organization (WTO) where the rules limit the options a country has. It may not, for example, make a trade arrangement favourable to one country but not others. In that regard the WTO incorporates some element of world planning and that can compromise the selfish interests of individual countries. A primary aim of the WTO has been to achieve market steadiness for traders and investors and the main device has been binding agreement on bounds for tariffs. For developed and transition economies more than 98% of products have been covered and more than 73% for developing economies. However, 100% of agricultural products are covered.

Banking

Inevitably, in the operation of a modern democracy the government becomes involved with international financial organizations with usually a serious effect on the government and the economy. The *International Monetary Fund* (IMF), to quote from their web site, "provides loans to member countries experiencing actual or potential balance of payments problems to help them rebuild their international reserves, stabilize their currencies, continue paying for imports, and restore conditions for strong economic growth, while correcting underlying problems." In acting out this role the IMF may impose onerous conditions on the government's financial management of its country. For example, following a public debt crisis in 2009 Greece had to seek a bail-out from the euro zone and the IMF. In fact there have been three bail-out programs, totaling around €300bn. Those loans had conditions attached: that Greece slash its public spending, and reform its corrupt, inefficient government bureaucracy. Although justified financially, the IMF has had a serious effect on the Greek government's freedom of movement.

The *Bank for International Settlements* (BIS) is a bank for the central banks of many nations. Its stated purpose is to help those banks achieve monetary and financial stability and to encourage international cooperation. It does financial analysis and generates statistics for the purposes of policy making, academic research and public debate. It also supports global regulatory standards and best supervisory practices for banks around the world. Its Basil Standards require the capital/asset ratio of internationally active commercial banks to be above a prescribed minimum international standard, to improve the resilience of the banking sector. This ratio enables commercial banks to lend out many times the amount of money that they possess, which in effect is a license for them to create money. With banks creating up to 80% of the money they lend out the effect throughout the economy is profound and for its part the BIS is arguably the most influential external organization for a government to deal with. Nevertheless, in this century (since 2013) the bank has 60 central bank members representing about 95% of the world's GDP.

The World Bank is an international organization dedicated to providing financing, advice and research to developing nations to aid their economic advancement. Its accomplishments are real and very significant in terms of improving the infrastructure and economies of developing countries. At the same time the World Bank, together with the BIS and IMF, has been fostering a uniform manner of banking around the world. The motives are stability, security for both the banks and their customers' deposits, and investment reliability for the benefit of investors.

Industrial commitments

Virtually all governments readily cooperate in the implementation of international industrial standards. These are published documents that establish requirements and procedures that are designed to maximize the safety and reliability of products, materials and services that people use. They are implemented in products used in nearly every part of our lives, from transport, aircraft, electronics to construction of buildings and infrastructure. They also fuel the development and implementation of technologies that become part of the way we live, work and communicate. An example of the benefit of standards is the Wi-Fi system that underpins wireless networking applications around the world, such as wireless access to the internet from our offices and homes, even from public places such as airports, hotels, restaurants, trains and aircraft.

One of the important benefits of international standards is that parts and electronics manufactured in different countries will fit together seamlessly. For international trade this feature is indispensable. It also has an indirect effect on investing and raising capital in that the products of a new factory, for example, will fit into the international picture.

Another influence, in the area of the labour force, is the trend of International Framework Agreements (IFA's) that attempt to reach uniform procedures for conducting negotiations over rights and privileges of union represented workers. These agreements apply particularly to international corporations' global supply chains. If, for example, a vehicle is to be assembled from parts made in different countries by company subsidiaries then labour conditions must be compatible. They include an element of socialism, as might be expected of unionized labour, by including mention of the social responsibility of business and referring to the UN declaration on rights. IFA's began in the 1980's and had reached 38 by 2005 as globalization continued.

Protection of the environment

In the past forty years there has been an increasing awareness of the destructive influence of human activity on the natural environment. As governments have turned their focus on this problem the fact that the scope of such problems crossed international boundaries required agreements between countries that were willing to cooperate on their amelioration, if not solution. Thousands of such agreements now exist, usually among two to several countries. At the same time some problems are widespread, even worldwide, and have resulted in multilateral agreements involving many countries. There are hundreds of these. The agreements are usually detailed and complex, involving a large amount of science and the technical work of sampling, analyzing, study of trends, comparing explanations and theories, and evaluating abatement processes and procedures. The subjects cover a wide range from water and air pollution to deforestation and its effect on oxygen production and the reduction of the habitat and population of some species. Complying with these agreements requires a large investment of time, people-power and money by governments and some industries and can seriously limit their freedom of action in relevant areas. Construction of oil pipelines is an example. The concern with environmental damage is serious enough that a political party- the Green Party- has arisen in several democracies for the express purpose of putting environmental protection first on a government's agenda. If they gain seats in the legislature environmental protection will be frequently argued in Parliament.

Ideology

Since the mid- twentieth century the advanced democracies have been carried along on a current of ideology. The most accurate name for it is socialist liberalism because it is a blend of socialism and liberalism, terms that were defined earlier (Party System). In Europe it is called social democracy, possibly because socialism is a bad word after the terror of extreme socialism in Eastern Europe and Russia under the Union of Soviet Socialist Republics. The method of social democracy has been to bring about by legislation, rather than by violent revolution, the harnessing of industry for the benefit of everybody, not just the owners of businesses.

In the post WWII period the socialist movement took to confiscating major industries to effect its goal of employing industry for its social purposes. A good example is Britain where the coal, steel and electricity generation industries were largely taken over by the national government. The eventual result was inefficiency as companies were artificially maintained in a changing economic environment, e.g., the demise of coal, where they would not have survived under the competition. These inefficiencies became an intolerable burden on the national economy and demonstrated the wayward trend of their industry from those of more progressive countries, e.g., Germany. The 1980's saw a trend away from this kind of socialism as the confiscated industries were returned to private ownership. In the 1990's even the former Soviet Union privatized its industries, albeit in a chaotic manner.

In our century the socialist-combined-with-liberal movement has been moving aggressively into training all people, with emphasis on students in school, in the tenets of the ideology. The prominent ones are:

- Model of the population- the ideology posits that every person is automatically a member of a social establishment called society and the role of government is to fashion this establishment into an ideal society. Basic assumptions are that every member is responsible for every other and the right course of action is decided per the old utilitarian concept from the eighteenth and nineteenth centuries which says that the right action is the one that does the most amount of good for the most number of people. Naturally, results and quality are measured on a group basis. The often heard phrase "social justice" could be such a case, appearing to mean justice measured on a group basis.

- Inclusiveness- the ideal society includes everyone. Therefore, all criteria that are used to differentiate people must be expunged. Accordingly, the ideology refuses to evaluate cultures, religions, sexual orientations, health condition, language, disposition to crime or personal habits, and this attitude is reflected in social and immigration policies. It is circulated through frequent messages from the government and cooperative media that try to mold common opinion. Law, social taboos, and even language have been created and disseminated, forbidding discrimination in any situation, even on private premises that the owner formerly had freedom to control.

- Control of assets- to create an ideal society it is necessary for governments to control all assets of the population as necessary, irrespective of ownership. This principle manifests in the taxation system which takes money from all citizens to satisfy the needs of the government in its regular operations and programs. The money taken is not calculated on a quid pro quo basis, however, but by formulas that take more from those who have more. The government's quest for money aims at where the money resides and the government believes it has the authority to take what it needs.

In other ways government overrides right of ownership in pursuit of its goal of establishing an ideal society. For example, in hiring and treatment of workers a business is required to abstain from discrimination on the basis of which group the person is associated with. In short, social democratic governments believe they have a mandate from the people to harness businesses as necessary to accomplish their social objectives.

- Fluid borders- the ideology embraces fluid borders on the tacit assumption that the people of the receiving country may not be selective as to whom they may admit. Accordingly, migrants and other illegal immigrants are admitted, often without even an interview. The rules are bent to the breaking point to accommodate any culture, religion, race, sexual orientation or even medical condition.

- Abortion- the ideology accords no rights to the child in the womb and allows a mother to abort the child at any time up to birth, at least in 61 countries that include 39% of the world's population where the law grants this license to the mother. In other countries the same prerogative applies for acceptable reasons and up to a specified time after conception. These countries contain about 60% of the world's population. (Figures from the Centre for Reproductive Rights)

- Capital punishment- it is not permitted for any type of crime, no matter how much the victim suffered or the motive of the perpetrator.

- Homosexuality- has the same value and status as heterosexuality. It is simply a choice. The population is frequently reminded of this by the government, the news and entertainment media and by teachers in schools and colleges. An annual parade helps. The messages are made more palliative by the guise of promoting equal rights but the rights were composed to fit the ideology.

The spread of socialist liberal ideology throughout the political, commercial, industrial and social arenas appears to have followed a well considered plan. Appointing supreme court judges on the basis of their concurrence with the ideology helped in implementing the ideology from the highest court in the land and this was done as the opportunity arose. A second key tactic was to take over academia, including all centers of learning from universities down to elementary school. In that way the next generation of adults would be indoctrinated in the ideology and would populate the centers of power in government, industry, and the media. The third tactic was to get the news and entertainment media on board with the ideology. If necessary, broadcast companies could be majority-purchased by government and told what to report and not report. All of these methods and more have been used across the lands of modern democracies with the result that socialist liberal ideology is as embedded as religion was in centuries past.

Administration of justice

In the fight against crime nearly all national governments have joined international organizations such as Interpol to allow cross referencing of databases and cooperation in the apprehension of criminals. Other arrangements for extradition of criminals try to ensure that fleeing the country is not a viable method of escaping justice. In addition there is the International Criminal Court (ICC) that prosecutes criminals regardless of the country where crimes were committed. The ICC is particularly skilled at prosecuting war criminals.

Since the invention two centuries ago of police forces controlled by local government it has probably happened that the force was occasionally persuaded to modify its conduct to support the government's agenda. In this era of social democracy the phenomenon has become somewhat common. For example, a police force may be instructed by the government to not disclose the race of a criminal being sought by the police. This protects the subject race from acquiring a bad reputation related to crime which could lead to resentment of that race and discrimination. Critics claim that such tactics reduce the efficiency of the police force but governments consider them necessary for achieving their goal of social harmony.

CHAPTER 2

Modern Democracies: Fault Lines

Structure

Design of governments in modern democracies is basically pragmatic. Those who designed them knew they wanted an organization that would govern the population effectively, efficiently and consistently through centuries with nobody taking over control of the government. What they gave little attention to was the source of authority for governments to direct people and their property and to simply take money from them. This issue was tackled by a few political philosophers in the eighteenth and nineteenth centuries, people like the English political theorists John Locke and Thomas Hobbes and the French "philosophe" Jean Jacques Rousseau. They all professed a concept of a social contract whereby the individual person surrendered some rights for protection by a government. Except for the United States of America, which was strongly influenced by Hobbes and Locke, most democracies took to heart Rousseau's concept of the social contract that included the idea of the *general will* which was the legitimizing force for government authority. That idea was simply that government action would accord with the expressed will of the majority of the population which presumably would result in the greatest good for the population as a whole. The fault line here is that governments assume the power to legislate in any area of human activity, disregarding rights that get in the way. The "majority will" concept therefore opened the door to abrogation of rights of an individual or a minority. Not surprisingly, the belief that satisfaction of the majority wants is sufficient for government action allows a tyranny by the majority.

Persistent complaints that representative democracies tended to trample over fundamental rights caused government ideologues to devise a tactic to deal with this embarrassing fault. They issued formal documents that told the population what rights governments would acknowledge. Of course, these declarations omitted any rights that did not support the government's ideology. For example, since modern democracies incorporate a large degree of socialism, charters of citizens' rights do not include rights over their property. The Canadian "Charter of Rights and Freedoms", which does not include the right to security of, nor freedom to control one's property, is one instance. The omission of property rights permitted governments to take people's money with impunity and to utilize their assets, like businesses and rental properties, for the government's purposes. The defensive argument that these purposes include the alleviation of sub-standard living conditions does not completely excuse the means, which is the disregard of the fundamental right to control one's property.

Another structural fault is that people elected into government have a set term in office, usually four or five years. They therefore approach their duties with a four or five year horizon. If they become involved in a longer project they know that they may not be there to account for the conduct of the project nor the results. This phenomenon is especially true in regard to persistent problems that have plagued the nation for many years. Politicians tend to feel that they can only work against these problems (and preferably be seen to do so) but actually solving them is not their responsibility. Exceptions to this modus operandi are extremely rare but there happens to be one at present in the form of US President Donald Trump who has the disposition that he is actually responsible for solving the problems. In this regard at least, he exhibits a trait that is required in proper government.

Yet, there is a partial saviour to this weakness in government. The civil service consists mostly of career men and women who remain there through changes of government after elections. They carry on with administrative procedures, dealing with the public and making progress on long term programs. They also constitute the great majority of people employed by the government. Their competence, honesty and dedication are primary factors in the effectiveness and efficiency of government. It may also explain the better performance of the advanced democracies and the inferior performance of politically, economically and/or socially backward democracies. In any case, better government will be achieved by supplying the right motivation to all staff in the support organizations to government (aka civil service). On the other hand, however, virtually guaranteeing an employee a job for life with protection from the consequences of neglect of responsibility, inattention to detail, bad decisions, duplicity and fear of taking initiatives is not proper motivational strategy. Yet, it is common in modern democracies.

Party System

The most damning criticism of the party system is that it subverts the basic process of democracy whereby elected representatives of the population come to the capital to insert the interests of their constituents into the discussion of proposed legislation. When they arrive they are required to uphold the policies of their party and if there is a difference with the preferences of their constituents the party must come first. If they refuse on any issue they will be promptly dismissed from the party and have to sit as an independent in the legislature. Their positions on pending legislation become irrelevant unless there is a tie in the voting. The net result is that the direction taken by the nation (or sub-jurisdiction) is determined by the majority party in the government while the preferences of the population come second. The fact that the ruling party (or coalition of parties) has a majority of seats in the legislature does not imply that they obtained a majority of votes, especially in a first-past-the-post election. Therefore, the program of the ruling party is not necessarily coincident with the preferences of the population. Policies on illegal immigrants and migrants have become a contentious example. The question of capital punishment is an abiding example.

With the power to control how the elected representatives from their party vote a party that has taken up a particular ideology has the means to implement it across the nation. This is exactly what has happened in the Western World and increasingly in the rest where socialist liberal ideology is the creed behind policy decisions by the government. This takeover would have been much more difficult if all elected representatives operated in accordance with their own consciences or if the upper house of a legislature was not partisan but instead evaluated pending bills objectively.

Another serious demerit of the party system is the spectacle, brought to the public by television, of inter-party wrangling and bickering in and out of the legislature. It is an image of wasted time and emotional energy. The citizen asks herself if this is why a representative was sent to the capital. It appears to be a game of politics with the goal being to make an opposing party look foolish. The serious business of governing requires time, energy and focus and suffers if any are in short supply. It suffers critically when parties are deadlocked in their opposing roles, a situation that has arisen in the United States, with partial government paralysis being the consequence.

Financial Management

In the weeks leading up to an election the competing political parties sell their programs with promises of more government benefits for the population. After the winner is elected the new government must find the money to pay for the election promises. Every conceivable tax will be examined for its potential to increase revenue. When that effort is exhausted the government will borrow the rest of what it needs. The process will be repeated in the next election and the one after that and after that with a consequent rise in taxes to the practical limit (intolerability) and then borrowing the remaining requirement. By the mid-1990's this process was clearly driving welfare state democracies toward insolvency as they contemplated the next step in borrowing which was to borrow the money to make the interest payments on the government's debt. It was like a homeowner increasing his mortgage every year to get the money to pay the interest on the mortgage. Countries in this predicament reduced spending to bring the budget into balance and stop the yearly increase in debt. Canada achieved this in 1997, the United Kingdom by 1998 and the United States by 2000, to name a few. In the next ten years growing economies allowed national debts to be reduced as a proportion of Gross Domestic Product (GDP) and servicing costs to be reduced correspondingly but also because of lower interest rates.

In late 2008 the financial crisis hit, changing the situation dramatically. An economic depression loomed unless money was thrown into the right places to stabilize banks and business profits, maintain liquidity and stimulate business investment. Consequently, governments borrowed again and heavily. Interest rates below 2% made it possible; so total debt rose enormously and is still rising. These debts leave governments with exposure to higher service charges if interest rates rise. That would cause a reduction in level of social programs or ever increasing debt or both. However it plays out one thing is certain: the debts will have to be repaid by future generations or at least the annual interest charges if that is all they can afford. It is an unfair burden to place on future generations because they will have to pay the cost of loans incurred by someone else.

These debts are at such a high level it is unrealistic to believe they can be repaid with money of the same value; they can only be repaid with money of less value. Therefore, they predicate future substantial inflation which will have a corresponding reduction in the buying power for those on fixed incomes. It would have the same result if wages did not keep pace with inflation which appears probable if the pattern of the last twenty years is a guide. These effects tend to move society toward a lower standard of living. In some democracies this effect is already felt.

A major reason why governments require so much money is because they are not careful spending it. That is because the people administering the government's purse have little personal incentive to obtain value for all money spent. Their primary motive is to do the purchasing task in a way that does not draw criticism. When everyone is so motivated there will be little criticism and little conscientious effort to minimize cost. In addition, if there is recourse to borrowing when costs exceed revenues then the incentive to keep those costs down is corrupted. How much will an employee try to minimize cost on a government expense when his/her supervisor stands ready to borrow money to cover overruns? The net result of deficit financing (more costs than money available) is inefficiency that compounds the problem.

Another questionable feature of modern democracies is that taxes are not based on the cost to government of the things being taxed. Tax on tobacco and alcohol products have already been discussed (Chapter 1). Add to that the tax on gasoline and other charges per vehicle. These are not calculated to cover the cost of the road system but on the basis of what the drivers will bear. If there was a correlation, however, it would be more evident of how much maintenance and new roads are enough and how much public transportation would make economic sense.

Influences on government

Some efforts to influence government decisions are beneficial and some are detrimental. They are beneficial when they bring to the deliberations facts, data, analyses, reactions and reasons that help the politicians to understand the ramifications of the issue. They are detrimental when they try to put the interests of a few people ahead of the interests of the population. Both of these types of influence happen in most democracies and the quality of the government is very much dependent on how much the first type outweighs the second. Some democracies are so corrupted by influence peddling that they actually are not fit to rule. Consequently, conversion to democracy is not a guarantee of economic or social prosperity. Successful democracy depends on honest politicians and honest government workers. To the degree these are lacking the democracy is a sham and a failure.

It should be remembered that extensive lobbying of a government will accumulate hours of time from the people elected to work on outstanding issues and legislation. When not used profitably the result is inefficiency. If the government is persuaded to spend money where it is not deserved it is waste. Both these evils can be found to some degree in every government, particularly when an elected politician believes he/she was elected to bring as much government money to his/her jurisdiction and never mind the morality of it. When politicians demand money for their re-election campaigns in return for promising favourable consideration to the lobbyists' clients, then it is a form of corruption that ruins the integrity of the democratic process. It is like a disease in government and difficult to cure.

The trend to global business operation, with the nod from governments that have been unduly influenced by rich and determined lobbies , favours multinational corporations but not the workers in the advanced democracies. They have seen factories moved to other countries where people work for much lower wages. With the factories went jobs, particularly good paying jobs and opportunity for advancement. The failure of wages to keep up with inflation is suspicious, tending to bring wages in the high paying countries down to world averages.

International Business Arrangements

Trade

In general, participation in international trade agreements will be excessive when the net result is damaging to a country's economy or people. Unfortunately, in some countries this fact has taken second place to the benefits to business elites, investor capitalists or just to unfettered commercial activity. In some instances trade flow has been set up to favour industry in one country at the expense of the importing country in terms of jobs and loss of factories. It is the situation that has aroused President Trump of the United States to take action against China, for example, because 60,000 factories in the

United States closed down since 2001 when China joined the World Trade Organization (WTO). To be fair, not all can be attributed to the rise of China (economically). There were the factors of automation and general decline in demand for US-made goods. Yet, between 4.2 and 4.7 million jobs were lost, to be replaced with lower paying service jobs. Despite the WTO's efforts to harmonize trade, serious distortions and hardship has occurred in some countries.

Banking

Starting in the 1970's the Bank for International Settlements (BIS) has persuaded its member governments to borrow money from private creditors, at interest, instead of from their central bank without interest. The theory was that borrowing from a central bank with the power to create money on its books would inflate the money supply and prices. The result of the change was that member governments have paid trillions of dollars (or equivalent) in service charges from taxpayer money. A case in point is Canada where the government switched, at the behest of the BIS, to borrow at interest. From 1975-2010 the Canadian taxpayer paid about $ 1.1 trillion in service charges (Helyer, Paul 2012). In 2019 the debt is growing at $2,000,000 per hour, every hour of the year. A sobering realization is that most of the borrowing is to obtain the money to pay the service charge on money previously borrowed. However justified, it is quite a burden on a country of 34+ million people.

Industrial commitments

The spread of international standards for manufacturing and building is no doubt admirable but failed to achieve a single system of weights and measures. Most of the world uses Le Systeme Internationale (SI) but the United States, Liberia and Myanmar use the old foot-pound-second system of measurement. Therefore, machines made in the USA, including vehicles, force mechanics to keep a second set of tools to repair them. In the scientific community conversion between units must often be made. It is a nuisance problem that is still waiting for a solution.

Protection of the environment

The world-wide fervour to protect the environment has countries that are minor polluters taking more remedial actions than countries that are major polluters. Equally, concern over ruining the habitats of threatened and endangered species is higher in some countries that do not have the species than in countries that do. These imbalances are an inter-government challenge that has yet to be resolved.

Ideology

Ever since people sat down to discuss what proper government should look like a certain approach was irresistible. It was generated by a dream of a disciplined, well working, safe and harmonious society. People like Thomas More, Edward Bellamy, Charles Fourier, H.G. Wells and others were inspired to write about utopias and, in the case of Mr. Fourier, to build a demonstration one in Indiana, USA (Brook Farm). Proper government would meet the aforementioned requirements and be just. Modern democracies went down the same road but in a more complex environment and in a more down-to-earth way.

However, their basic intention became, in due course, similar: to create an ideal society.

Implicit in the approach was the view of the population as a group to be regulated as necessary to achieve the total result. The regulation takes the form of laws from the legislature, policies for government operation, and procedures, both internal to government and external for interface with the public. In their application they can bump against rights of the individual person and this is a problem. The observation depends, of course, on the belief that natural, 'a priori' rights exist. Denial was an early tactic of nineteenth century liberals and socialists, e.g., Jeremy Bentham who claimed "Right is the child of law, from 'laws of nature' come imaginary rights..." Although two centuries have passed since that utterance it is still an attitude in modern democracies. The next chapter will present a theory showing these rights to be very real but even without that theory many people feel intuitively that they are basically autonomous, with innate rights.

The feeling comes from the blatant fact that every human being came into the world by the same indiscriminate process of Nature/God which puts every person on the same footing. Consequently, every person is an entity, not part of one unless he/she chooses to be. This is the basic state of human life or indeed that of any animal. The socialist view is that every person is automatically, from birth, a part of an entity consisting of human society. This view is an abstraction from the basic state but claims absolute validity. Its origin is probably the recognition of a cause-effect relationship between a person living among his/her kind and the interdependence that usually occurs. The effect is more pronounced as self-reliance is replaced by inter-reliance as happened from the industrial revolution. People worked in factories to earn enough money to buy what they needed. Socialism arose in response to deprivation caused by workers earning insufficient money to purchase their needs and in poor working conditions that resulted from negligence. As clear as these reasons were and still are to a lesser degree, they do not alter the fact that socialism is a contrived model of mankind that is not the basic condition of a person among his/her kind but is rather a radical excursion from it. Socialism's answer to the question, "Is a person born into a situation or into a club?" is the latter and the club is "society". Any theory that arises in contradiction to this social model is apt to be called a radical theory, which is arguably a backwards interpretation of reality. This book is no doubt an example.

Returning to rights, when a government does acknowledge a natural right (seldom) it claims that it is inferior to the government's right to mould society (the government does not use that term) but the idea that rights can be ranked contradicts the concept of rights as absolute within their purview. Nevertheless, it is a tactic that leaves the individual with no recourse. The power and authority of government is generally accepted for the benefits that result but the occasional collision with fundamental rights has not been fully reconciled. The following are basic or recurring rub points.

- Property rights

The taking of money from citizens under taxation formulas that are far away from a quid pro quo basis conflicts with the owner's natural right to security of what he/she owns. Quid pro quo means that a person pays for the value of what he/she gets, like the itemized bill from a business. If money is taken without returning something of commensurate value this transgresses the person's right to security of his/her money.

Secondly, a common view among people is that they have the right to control what they own. Governments ignore this right when they lay down requirements to businesses that forbid them from exercising prejudice in hiring, acquiring as tenants, or serving or not serving in one's place of business. Governments claim that these restrictions are to protect the right of people to freedom from discrimination but that right was invented as a support for the aim of including everybody in the vision of an ideal society. It is not an absolute right that has historical roots. Rather, the historical precedent is that the owner of a property has the right to choose who to admit to his property, based on any reason. Also, the owner may be selective as to whom to serve and whom not. Incidentally, the concern that being selective may unacceptably disrupt the working of society is ameliorated by the prerogative of business customers to avoid a business that practices discrimination against a particular group. In any event, the question of rights is not resolved as supporters of socialist liberal democracies contend but it is instead controversial and possibly in reverse order.

- Inclusiveness

The objective of inclusiveness has given birth to a sub-concept of universalism that turns a blind eye to all distinguishing features among people of various creeds, customs, sexual orientations, etc., and equates them all. The concept defies reasonable standards that could be used to evaluate cultures and creeds, such as respect for the individual person, for his and her right to manage their own lives, or for other fundamental rights. By these measures all cultures and religions do not appear to be equal. Sexual orientations are not equal in their role of continuing the population into the future.

- Fluid borders

Socialist liberal ideology ignores the right of a country's population to choose who they will welcome as permanent residents and who they will refuse. Instead, it posits that everyone should be admitted because, under the doctrine of universalism, all people are equal in all respects. Therefore, there are no grounds for refusing arrivals at the country's borders. The implication is profound. It implies that borders are meaningless and the concept of a country as the preserve of a group of people descended from those who created it and were ready to defend its essence and territory is superseded by a grander vision of a global community of diverse cultures, religions and races, all somehow living in harmony. The vision has the considerable obstacle that the things that people believe are not always compatible, nor equally meritorious. At the level of culture, language, religion or tribe the adherents are reluctant to mix. Difference in religion split India into two countries after 1948 independence from Britain. The Balkan countries are set up more or less along tribal lines. In Canada most of the French speaking population lives in the province of Quebec. In Europe there are many recent Muslim enclaves. These demonstrate the human predilection to live among one's kind. The idealists who want their country to be home to a truly diverse population could be heading toward a Balkanized country that lacks solidarity and has different degrees of loyalty depending on the community.

There is also the basic nature of the world's population. It is composed of a variety of racial, ethnic, tribal, religious and language groups that evolved almost in isolation from one another until the arrival of steam powered ships and locomotives only a century and a half ago. They have their own gods, superstitions, philosophies, customs and ingrained attitudes. They also have different levels of average intelligence, according to scientists in the field (Lynn, R & Meisenberg, G 2010), which vary over a range of 48 points on the intelligence quotient (IQ) scale. It is these differences that probably account for the differences in political, economic, social and intellectual achievements among the groups and suggest that an individual person has the best chance in his/her life if competition is only among his/her kind. Mixing groups together will probably result in social problems and economic stratification. Nevertheless, it is what the ideology is promoting.

Besides these practical considerations there is a suspicion that the campaigns of the socialist liberal establishment to create diverse societies in Europe and America are part of a plan to destroy the hegemony of the white European populations even in their own countries. Extremists in the establishment blame that hegemony for the economic disparity of non-white groups on both continents. Scientists, however, blame innate factors in the poorer groups, such as education, attitudes, useful training, cultural and/or religious conditioning, personal conscientiousness and intelligence (Ceci, S.J. & Williams, W.M. 1997). The socialist liberal establishment believes that the combination of the world's races, ethnic groups, tribes and religions, in what they call a "post-national state", is an act of construction but it also can be seen as an act of wholesale destruction. Yet, the movement has attracted an incredible number of supporters from among the target group. The worrisome thing is that the movement may be taking the human race down the wrong road and it is practically irreversible.

• Abortion

Those who support abortion accord no rights to the baby in the womb. This is one of the two central issues in the abortion debate. The other one is whether the baby is part of the mother's body or not. On this latter question it is very clear when the baby emerges from the womb that he/she is a new body, the product of Nature's/God's way of procreating the species. The essence cannot be different when the baby is in the womb. Furthermore, the baby is connected to the mother only by an umbilical cord. The opponents of abortion accept that the baby, even in the womb, is a human being and therefore has those rights that every human being naturally has. The first of these is the right to security of its life and abortion is therefore the grossest violation of that right. The views are irreconcilable which suggests a referendum as the right way forward but a way that the socialist liberal establishment is reluctant to take.

• Homosexuality, transgenderism, etc.

The next chapter includes a treatise on fundamental rights which shows that a person has a right to manage his/her life in all respects. This would include choosing a homosexual lifestyle. Since that is a fundamental right other people have no justification for persecuting a person who makes that choice and laws against homosexuality are certainly wrong. For a person who knows real fundamental rights there is no question about this and no need for repeated assertion of the right to choose homosexuality. Yet, the amount of homosexuality included in news stories, entertainment on film, advertising and school curricula appears way out of proportion to the issue of rights and to the proportion of the population that is homosexual (less than 5% per UCLA Williams Institute). The reason for such exaggerated attention is that the intent of the socialist liberal establishment is bigger than the issue of rights. The ideology posits that homosexuality is equal in value to heterosexuality and therefore should be equal in status. This was implicit in the claim by some governments that a homosexual couple was just as qualified to get married as a heterosexual one. The equality that governments are aiming for is a manifestation of their belief that an ideal society includes everyone on an equal basis. It seems to be an admirable goal but there is a fault. If a population devalues family life as it raises the value of homosexual life then that population will head toward extinction. That is already happening in the advanced democracies where the birth rate is well below the 2.1 required to sustain a population and has been since the mid-1970's. Therefore it is plain that continuation of the population requires that family life remains as mainstream humanity but in the continuing social-political environment it is de-emphasized.

- Same sex marriage

It is advocated by the ideology but is faulty on the rights that support that initiative. In their zeal to include everyone in the workings of society governments have assumed the attitude that marriage is a generic thing like mating. But mating is a natural affair, only requiring the agreement of the two parties involved, i.e., no permissions and no formalities. Even animals mate. Marriage, however, is not a generic thing; it is a man-made institution for the purpose of formalizing the union of a man and a woman. That is how it was created millennia ago and how it functioned for thousands of years in virtually every culture on earth. Those jurisdictions that unilaterally expanded marriage to include homosexual couples also, at the same time, cancelled the right of the heterosexual population to a unique institution for uniting a man and a woman. This went unnoticed by the news media, the public and the supreme courts. Instead, the politicians did what the ideology demanded which, in many cases, was what party leaders told them to support.

In recent decades the ideology has been pushed aggressively, on the premise that its view of human rights is correct and definitive. The counter views on property rights, abortion, immigration and same sex marriage, although reasonable, are labeled "right wing" or "far right", often ridiculed and invariably dismissed. There is increasing anger and consternation as the self-righteous attitudes emanating from government and the media become more apparent even to the usually apathetic public. Numerous web sites that challenge the politically correct agenda have developed in recent years and have picked up followers. In Europe populist political parties that arose in response to governments making decisions that appeared to go against what citizens want, have been gaining ground with each election.

What has become especially alarming, to parents in particular and other interested parties, is the spread of homosexual and transgender ideology into elementary schools. Striped homosexual flags flying from poles at some of these schools is a clear indication of what the ideologues are doing. They are indoctrinating children from first grade in their controversial ideology. In high schools and colleges the indoctrination continues with the apparent intention of cementing the ideology into future generations. Many people have become concerned or alarmed at such forceful incursion into their choices for their children and objection has steadily become vocal and better organized. It appears that serious division is opening up between the politically correct group and the otherwise apathetic group that has woken up. Social division could lead to political division and that has the potential for serious violence.

Administration of justice

Although the administration of justice is intended to be a separate branch of government that operates independently the government is able to effectively control its operation by appointing the head of the branch and judges to the Supreme Court. This control was evident in the move by most democratic governments to abolish capital punishment. It apparently was a purely ideological decision that subverted justice to a vision of an ideal society. This claim is, of course, dependent on a definition of justice, which is very hard to find but intuitively it must surely mean that a person gets what he/she deserves. That notion of justice was put aside in favour of objectives for society as a whole but occasionally the dissatisfaction of victims or their families is heard.

A second case is that of the unilateral expansion of marriage by governments to include homosexual couples, as discussed previously. The fault in the justice system is that supreme courts did not uphold the right of the heterosexual population to have an exclusive institution for formalizing the union of a man and a woman in a conjugal relationship. If they did it would have been necessary for governments to get the permission of the heterosexual population before opening it to others.

Also worrisome is the influence of government over the police forces. These forces supposedly operate under a mandate to enforce the laws passed in the legislature but are being used by government to support their management of society as a whole. Some questionable practices have arisen, such as not charging offenders who are members of a sensitive immigrant group, or not prosecuting them if they are charged. A sensational case in England was revealed in the "Independent Inquiry into Child Exploitation in Rotherham (1997-2013)". Published on 26 August 2014, the report claimed that an estimated 1,400 children had been sexually exploited in Rotherham between 1997 and 2013. The report revealed that children as young as 11 were "raped by multiple perpetrators, abducted, trafficked to other cities in England, beaten and intimidated". Most of the perpetrators were identified as Pakistani Muslim men. The scope of the crimes was appalling, as was the scope of the failures of the Rotherham Borough Council, the South Yorkshire Police and the Crown Prosecution Service to protect the girls (mostly white), apprehend the perpetrators or charge them with crimes. Several police officers, it was reported, were reluctant to arrest perpetrators for fear of being accused of racism. Some were told specifically not to mention the ethnic group of the perpetrators. However, the general public has a right to expect the police forces to pursue criminals impartially, thoroughly and efficiently and to know what immigrant groups are seriously misbehaving after arriving.

The foregoing are the systemic problems embedded in modern democracies and impair its proper functioning going forward. The following chapters propose a solution to these problems using the method of finding undeniable principles on which to build proper governments.

CHAPTER 3

Proper Government

Theory

In facing the faults with modern democracies people have two ways in which to react. The first is to accept the faults as the price for the good features of democracies and the second is to imagine a different kind of government that does not include those faults in its design. Few people think along those lines, some remembering Winston Churchill's famous epithet, "... democracy is the worst form of government, except for all the others that have been tried from time to time..." Yet, if a government that is designed to avoid the worst structural and operational faults of its predecessors also has a logically determined, unquestionable right to rule then we could call such a government "proper government". The idea has been developed into a full concept that appears in the following as the second treatise in political science. The first is about what the government governs. At the highest level it governs a country, an entity so familiar to most people that it is taken for granted. A perusal of the world globe, with its coloured patchwork of countries, may stimulate an open mind to wonder how they came about and what principles sustain them. The answer to those questions is given below as a tract in political science.

Theory of a Country

The term "country", in the political sense, is generally understood to be an area of the planet that is politically independent.   Besides this phenomenological view there is the question of what a country is in concept, including how a country is created. A genuine country is created by a particular group of people who, for their own reasons, claim a specific area of the planet as their own. The borders are carefully defined on maps utilized for the purpose if such maps exist. The reasons could be common ancestry, tribal affiliation, race, religion, geographical factors or indeed any factors that give the people the feeling that the land they occupy is theirs. Those who are willing to support the exclusive claim to territory, defending its borders against challengers as and when necessary, could be termed countrymen or citizens if there is a government. Implicit in the claim is the intention of approving or not anyone who wants to enter the country for permanent settlement. If this is not done, there would be no real purpose to the claim of exclusivity and no real country.

A few countries have been artificially created by powers outside the region in question. This was done without obtaining the commitment by the majority of the population to take on the responsibility and burden of being a citizen. It should not be surprising then that in some instances internal dissension caused such countries to fall apart or they were easily conquered by a more intact and organized enemy.

Examples are in Africa (Central African Republic), the Middle East (Iraq, Syria, Lebanon) and Europe (Czechoslovakia).

When a country is acknowledged by the majority of the world's population, which itself is grouped by countries, then a basically stable assembly of countries is in place and a world map showing definite countries is possible. This does not imply that a country will not be attacked by an aggressor but the aggressor will have to deal not only with the defenses of the target country but with the wrath of the majority of countries, some of which may be allied with the target country. When a country has a government whose jurisdiction covers the whole country then the country qualifies as a state in the world's legal system of political standing. Although limited here to this context the term "state" is often used by news media in other contexts. The term "country" runs deeper, being a visceral expression by a large group of people of the territorial instinct for land possession. However, it can take a large amount of work, determination, sacrifice and hope to keep the idea of a particular country alive, but only by diluting the idea and causing it to evaporate can a country be destroyed. Such forces have done so in the past- Yugoslavia in the 1990's for example- and are active today in South Sudan and almost destroyed Somalia.

To complete the subject a clarification of the term "nation" which is sometimes used inappropriately for country is required. According to the Oxford dictionary of English a nation is a large body of people united by common descent, history, culture, or language, inhabiting a particular state or territory. To that could be added the quality that they exhibit the will to live together. In reality the territory they occupy could be in part of a country or parts in different countries. For example, the Kurdish nation of people occupies territory in Turkey, Iraq, Iran and Syria. Aboriginal nations in North America exist in parts of the host countries (USA and Canada). When a nation has its own country and national government it is called a "nation-state".

*****

The Theory of a Country provides a clear, definite notion of what a country is, which is important because a country is the platform on which any form of government is built. Besides its place in the concept of proper government this theory has become necessary in this century because so many politicians have lost sight of the meaning of a country and of firm borders around it. They preach disregard for illegal entries and indiscriminate mixing of different cultures, religions and values as though the existence of a distinct country is no longer meaningful or useful. By any calculation, however, the history of a country should have interest as a part of the human story.

On the base of an existing country the people may create a government and if it is a proper government it will conform to the second treatise which follows.

Theory of Proper Government

The base case of the formation of proper governance would proceed along the following theoretical lines.

- A group of people establish control over a demarcated region of the planet and form a country.

- The people responsible- they could be called countrymen- will likely conclude that a central authority is required to organize and manage defense forces to repel invaders and to process transient people at the borders for acceptability.

- A logical extension of its role is to provide security within the borders, that is, security for the person and property of every inhabitant which is a fundamental requirement for a viable country.

- Another logical extension is to protect and preserve the natural environment for the benefit of present residents and their descendants.

- The residents therefore create a government for these purposes.

In this base case each person is coming from the raw state of nature to the establishment of a country, so it can reasonably be assumed that he/she will want all his/her rights protected in exchange for assuming the burden of supporting the government's efforts because protection of rights ensures, firstly, the security of one's person and possessions and secondly, the personal freedom that should go with equality of status. This supposes that every man and woman is a free agent, possessed of certain rights that naturally go with a person. The theory of these rights appears later in this chapter. The contract between a person and the government, whether written or not, is that he/she will support the government in exchange for protection of his/her rights. Those who accept this contract may be called citizens.

Since the government is created by citizens then they own the government collectively. Therefore, the government is accountable to the citizens. Furthermore, key positions in the government, specifically those that determine the direction the government takes in fulfilling its duties, as well as on issues of the day, can be staffed by people elected by the citizens. In such elections, which should occur at regular intervals of reasonable duration, every citizen has equal status (as co-owner) and therefore an equal vote.

With the government in place the citizens may employ it for other purposes as long as the rights of any citizens are not transgressed. They may, for example, have the government create and maintain a system of currency to facilitate trade. They may have the government create and enforce rules and procedures governing use of the roads, seaways and air travel to maintain order and safety. In many other ways the government can be usefully employed to regulate human activity to protect rights, improve utility, and ensure safety. The government may regulate the utilization of the natural environment for the purpose of protecting and preserving it and also to provide safe access for the country's inhabitants.

The main government may create sub-levels of government to improve effectiveness. Each of these sub-governments will have less scope in geography and number of people and will be better able to focus on regional character, whether that is natural features or people of a different tribe, culture, language, religion or common occupation. The central government's mandate of protecting every person's rights will normally carry over to sub-jurisdictions but there may be exceptions. Within the framework of a rights-protected political system it is possible to have sub-jurisdictions where rights are traded by citizens for some benefit that is very important to them. It could be material benefit like guarantee of subsistence needs and medical needs, or spiritual benefit like a religious society or ideological realization such as a socialist system. Any such jurisdictions should be defined by a charter that includes what rights must be surrendered and to what limits. Some rights may not be surrendered so that an individual is not taken advantage of, however. These would include the right to security of one's life and limb, freedom from forced confession or manipulation or unjustified confinement, to name a few. As with a monastery or convent every person in such jurisdictions must be a volunteer and have the option of leaving.

Governments that conform to this theory can be called proper government and conversely, those that do not are improper governments. Unfortunately, nearly all the governments in the world at this time (2019) fall into the latter category because they deliberately ignore some fundamental rights that some or all of the people have, depending on the case. The fundamental rights referred to here are those that can be shown by an impartial analysis to be intrinsic to every person in the world (covered later in The Theory of Human Rights). They do not include rights invented for a purpose. In the most serious cases of abuse a few governments actually murder, torture and falsely imprison some of its citizens. Even in the Western World, which considers itself to be a champion of human rights, the disregard of property rights is systematic. Governments take the money of citizens to pay for an ideological program supported by a nominal majority. For the same reason they ignore the citizen's sole right to control his/her property. However, since true fundamental rights are absolute the majority does not have sufficient authority to ignore them. In all cases of abrogation of fundamental rights, the government-citizen contract described earlier is broken and consequently the government loses its right to rule to a matching extent.

In summary, *proper government* is one that conforms to the following requirements.

- Government is, in principle, a creation of the citizens for their purposes.

- Government is owned by the citizens collectively and is therefore accountable to them.

- Government operates per a contract (usually tacit) with every citizen whereby the citizen supports the government in its efforts in exchange for protection of his/her rights.

- The citizens have the right to elect people into the government as a means to control government action and performance against its purposes.

The political constitution of a proper government will not deviate from the above principles.

****

The above theory has a number of worthy features that explain government where it has not been explained before. The first is the clarification of where a government properly comes from and the reason it may command obedience in those areas involved with its purposes. Importantly, those purposes are not decided by government members, nor by the legislature alone, but must be ratified by the governed population. In practice, a proposal would be presented to the population, complete with scope, organization, description of operation and definite budget, for their consideration before voting on it. If the regular payments to each individual (discussed later) will be reduced by the cost the amount must be disclosed in the information.

The theory explains why a government is accountable to those governed and why it must set up functional organizations, including police forces. All of these are required to fulfill the government's purposes and to protect people's rights. The theory also explains why leaders in the government must be elected and why every citizen has an equal vote regardless of gender or other distinguishing features.

Some features of the theory are revolutionary in concept and implication. They are transcendent over the total government organization and provide philosophic guidance and support. For instance, the concept of government's right to rule, being based on a contract between each citizen and the government as explained earlier, implies that each citizen is an equal shareholder in the government. Therefore, the government must serve the individual first and the group second, not the other way around, just as a public corporation would. Factors such as race, gender, ethnic group, tribe, religion, economic status and educational level are irrelevant. If a population can be convinced of this fact then a harmonious society is probable. The government-citizen arrangement implies that the government is agent and its role is to provide a framework in which the citizen may live free as long as other people's rights are respected and laws, which essentially protect rights, are obeyed. Another instance is the application of majority rule. In a proper government the will of the majority applies only to things that are owned in common and does not apply to anything at all as it presently does in nearly all legislatures. What is owned in common is all that Nature provided and the government itself. That is why citizens may employ the government for any purpose that does not infringe on people's rights.

Of course, proper government, as described here, will not please many people. In particular, those people who want to live by an ideology such as a religious prescription or the socialist liberal full society model that is presently so popular, may be discontent. The foregoing theory provided the means for accommodating their aspirations. It mentioned that among the sub-levels of government there may be political jurisdictions that are defined by charters specifying what rights must be surrendered and to what limits because this is the primary aspect dividing government by ideology from government by rights. There was the proviso that certain rights, such as the right to personal security, right to due process under law, and the right to leave are considered inalienable rights and therefore cannot be surrendered.

It is worth noting in passing that while proper government can accommodate deviations from a strictly rights based social-political environment the reverse is not true. Societies that manifest an ideology such as the present socialist liberal or restrictive religious societies cannot accommodate the requirements of proper government because the surrender of rights is assumed, not volunteered. People may have some of their money taken, not on a quid pro quo basis, but to satisfy the plan of an ideology. A person may lose his or her life for renouncing a religion. Under proper government a person could agree to have his/her money taken on other than a quid pro quo basis but a person could not subject his/her life to forfeiture for an optional religious belief.

Under proper government a person has total freedom to control what he/she owns as long as the rights of others are not offended. Also, the security of what is owned is protected by the government. This implies that government may not simply take what it decides it needs to carry out a program. Rather, it collects what it has earned from providing a secure environment and through investments and can finance programs from these revenues but not levy extra taxes to pay for programs. The earning from providing the economic system is in the form of tax on income, estimated as the value of the government's contribution to each $100. of the worker's earnings in a similar manner to a gambling casino that calculates its proportion of bets made.

Taxation on a quid pro quo basis is not the only way in which the proper government model differs from social democracy. Other tenets of that ideology are not incorporated because they are based in optional beliefs and are therefore disqualified from a general government framework. Important omissions or differences are below.

- As much as practical tax is designed to recover government cost attributable to the subject matter and may include a reasonable profit.

- Per the "Theory of a Country" the citizens of the country have the right to approve or not any foreigner wanting to enter the country, especially on a permanent basis. Any criteria may be applied.

- Family life remains at the centre of civilization. It brings new people into the world replacing those who die and in so doing it provides a natural purpose and destiny for men and woman. There may be exceptions to the tax and family life provisions in sub-jurisdictions that are defined by a charter that otherwise specifies these matters. This was mentioned earlier.

The most fundamental way in which the theory of government differs from social democracy is the acceptance of "a priori" fundamental rights instead of these rights being only what is granted by government. Moreover, their veracity and applicability is judged to be valid. The rights are explained in the third treatise which fills a gap in the foregoing theory.

The Theory of Human Rights

The idea that every human being has fundamental rights has been around for millennia because of the instinctive recognition, often clouded by cultural conditioning, that all persons came into the world by the same indiscriminate process of nature and therefore have equal status as human beings. Even animals have this instinct among their kind. The fact that every person has the faculties to sustain an independent, autonomous being further substantiated this recognition. In addition, it was seen that ownership conferred rights. These observations on the basic conditions of human life can form the base on which a complete theory of fundamental rights can be constructed.

The method used is to deduce rights from a person's fundamental status and from natural ownerships. The effort progresses from the axioms stated above to inescapable conclusions. Consequently, the rights so discovered are absolute. Furthermore, since the axioms are as true for a woman as a man the conclusions and resulting rights apply equally to a woman as to a man. They also do not distinguish human beings by race, culture, tribe, religion or any other apparent factor and are therefore universal, meeting the requirement for true fundamental rights.

Self-sovereignty

The equal status of every person as a human being precludes a person from unilaterally assuming control over another. Accordingly, every person has the sole right to control himself/herself, a right that can be termed self-sovereignty. It could also be said that a person owns himself/herself but not in the sense that this ownership can be transferred because it is innate to the person and therefore inalienable.

Ownership of what one creates

When a person creates something he/she brings into existence something that did not exist before or changes the configuration or condition of something already existing into a new thing or condition. It is a manifestation of the person's existence and the cause of the effect. Other people may have contributed in the act of creation but would not have ever produced it without the participation of the person whose intent and movement caused the effect. (To be the cause without the intent is usually classified as an accident). Being the indispensable agent, the subject person has the strongest claim to ownership. The other people who contributed in some way can have a claim, however, commensurate with the value of their contribution. If another person provided materials their claim is equal to the value of the materials in their former state.

Equal claim on nature

A corollary of the fact that all people have equal status as human beings is that the claim of each person on what nature provided is equal to any other's which produces ownership in common. With all the world divided into countries and with the assets of a country consisting of much more than nature's endowment it is not feasible to apply the principle on a worldwide basis. However, it follows that within a country all that nature provided is owned in common by all the permanent residents.

Ownership of animals

The natural state of animals is to run free in the wild. Yet, down through human history animals have been utilized for food, milk, laborious tasks, materials for garments and just as pets. When animals are viewed as a resource they are subject to the principle above, that is, everyone has an equal claim on them. It is possible for a person or group to, in effect, own animals through an arrangement with the affected community. Since the community will have the power of decision it may specify conditions such as: providing adequate food and drink, humane living conditions, refraining from physical abuse and so on. As a minimum the community will invariably require that the "owners" take responsibility for the animals.

The above logical development has produced four natural rights accruing from natural ownerships. Since they are founded on indisputable, general principles they are absolute and universal. The natural rights are:

a) A person is sovereign of himself/herself.

b) A person owns what he/she creates.

c) The permanent residents of a country own in common all that nature provided.

d) A person or group may, in effect, own animals through an arrangement with the affected community whereby, as a minimum, the owners take responsibility for the animals.

These rights generate subsidiary rights that are more specific and therefore more enforceable.

Personal security

Natural right (a), when understood as self-ownership, implies security and inviolability of one's person. This means that no one may assault another in any way without justification. An assault on the body could be an attack intended to cause pain, injury or discomfort and would include assault by any means, such as object, light, sound or anything else that would affect the senses. Assault on the mind would include unwelcome messages, invasions of privacy and attempts to control the mind, including the indoctrination of susceptible minds.

Freedom of conscience

Natural right (a) also includes ownership of one's mind which confers the right to evaluate and choose what to believe. This applies especially to optional beliefs, such as religion, superstitions, political ideology, contentious social theories and unverified reports on events, to name important ones. This right prohibits any person or group from imposing his/their optional belief onto another person, even in close relationships such as marriage or family. It does allow a person to practise his/her beliefs in premises that he/she has the right to control but is subject to the control of others in this regard in premises owned by others, including premises or areas that are owned in common by the population.

Right to manage one's life

Right (a) creates the right to manage one's life. This includes freedom to choose one's associates which includes in turn whom to marry, friendships, memberships in organizations and so on. Managing one's life includes choice of employer, where to live, customs, manner, style and habits. It includes the choice to follow one's sexual orientation, or even to change one's body in the process of changing one's gender. A person may choose to remain in the bosom of one's family, community, culture, religion, country or to remove himself/herself from any or all.

Ownership of what one creates whether in service to himself/herself or to others

Since right (b) is absolute it applies whether a person creates for himself/herself or for others. In the latter case the creation may be a gift, which will transfer ownership when given, or for compensation. The compensation should logically be based on the market value of the creation, even in regular employment situations. On receipt of payment the ownership will transfer to the payer.

Security of property

Right (b) states that a person owns what he/she has created which means the sole right to control it. This right would be transgressed if another person were to assume possession (steal), utilize, modify, damage or prevent access to the thing owned. The right to security of property applies to the new owner when ownership is transferred through trade or donation.

Access to nature

Right (c) implies that every person must have equal access to nature. Implicit in this right is the freedom for a person to obtain his/her subsistence needs from nature as mankind has done since the beginning. These rights may be subject, however, to regulations on access and use of the natural environment because of the common ownership of same by the whole population and the exercise of the majority will.

Entitlement to land

By right (c) every permanent resident of a country has an equal claim on all the land within the country. When it comes to utilization of this land it follows that every resident is entitled to an equal amount of land, measured by value. Because future generations may be more numerous but have the same entitlement then a portion of the land should be held in reserve for them. Therefore, it is not necessary, nor appropriate to distribute all the land in the country at a given time.

Exploitation of natural resources

Right (c) means, in effect, that every permanent resident of a country is an equal shareholder of all the country's natural resources. Therefore, when a person or group extracts a natural resource as a business then he/she/they must buy out the equity of every shareholder before selling the resource in a market.

Control of animals by regulation

Right (d) implies the control of animals by formal, general regulations put in place by the affected community and applying to the owners of animals.

Summary

The identified natural rights (a) to (d) plus the subsidiary rights comprise the fundamental rights that every person in the world has. They are listed following.

Natural rights

- A person is sovereign of himself/herself.

- A person owns what he/she creates.

- The permanent residents of a country own in common all that nature provided.

- A person or group may, in effect, own animals through an arrangement with the affected community whereby, as a minimum, the owners take responsibility for the animals.

Subsidiary rights

- Right to personal security and inviolability.

- Right to choose one's beliefs.

- Right to manage one's life.

- Right of ownership over what one creates, whether in service to himself/herself or others.

- Right to security of what one owns.

- Right of access to the natural environment, subject to rules on its care and use.

- Entitlement of every permanent resident of a country to an equal portion of available land, measured by value.

- Right of every permanent resident of a country to compensation for natural resources extracted for eventual sale in a market.

- Right to own animals, subject to regulations imposed by the affected community.

Author's note: there is a more elaborate description of the theory and its application in my book *Human Rights, What Are They Really?*, Published by Bradich Books in 2008.

Certain observations and qualifications should be stated about the theory.

- Conceivably, there could be more subsidiary rights derived from the natural rights.

- The theory contains no rights invented for a purpose because the approach taken was simply to discover what fundamental rights went with a person, i.e., are implicit with the reality of a person.

- Being absolute and universal the rights stand against any person or group regardless of what authority they claim. That includes the will of the majority.

- Every man-made thing has an owner which makes for a market in man-made goods.

- The rights allow freedom of action in various areas on the assumption that the subject is of sound mind. If not, then others may override the subject for his/her own good.

- The rights of a group are the sum of the rights of the constituent members, no less and no more.

* * * *

The above treatise completes the theoretical foundation for the construction of a proper government. It therefore lacks no guidance on what the government is there for and what is covered by its contract with each citizen. The government can also be confident that the rights it is obliged to protect are valid, permanent and the same for everyone, male or female. Furthermore, they can be defended as absolute and universal by The Theory of Human Rights which is an objective, discursive exposition of real human rights. This theory replaces existing doctrines of rights that took the wrong approach by simply composing rights to support a vision of an ideal society, yet claiming that these fitted the definition of human rights as intrinsic to every human being. This difference in the concept of fundamental rights is a basic divide between modern democracies and proper government. The divide is widened by the different status of rights in the government's plan. With a proper government the protection of rights is paramount whereas in a socialist liberal democracy (aka social democracy) the design of society is paramount and rights are reconfigured to suit.

The theory of rights informs government on the protection of the environment. In the formation of government as well as in the protection of rights the government acquires guardianship of the natural environment, firmly implanting its responsibility and authority to manage it for its limited utilization and, at the same time, sustainability so that it will be available for future generations. The authority applies within the entire country and also supports government action, in concert with other governments under international consensus, to control the exploitation of natural resources in the world's oceans and the Antarctic continent.

The theory also resolves several contentious issues of our time. The first is property rights. It has been well understood, not only among humans but animals too, that ownership confers the right to securely possess and control the thing owned. The theory clarifies that ownership accrues to the creator of the subject thing and this is true in any situation. A common situation in the modern world is the employment of people in business. What the people create that is of value, whether tangible or intangible, is owned by the person(s) who created it. Their compensation should therefore be for transferring ownership to the business. A point of caution, however: in implementing this principle it is vitally important to identify exactly what was created and the amount (production). The employee compensation should also include the duties required by affiliating with the business, such as allotting certain hours of the week to the business' obligations, maintaining confidences, loyalty and upholding the business' good name. A third component should complete the compensation and that is for bearing responsibilities on the job. All three components respect the man's or woman's time, production and carrying of responsibility.

The right of the population's common ownership over all that Nature provides begets a right to a dividend from the exploitation of any natural resource, as mentioned earlier. A business that extracts valuable commodities from above or below ground must buy out the equity of owners before selling the material in a market. Consequently, every man, woman and child should receive regular dividend payments from all the businesses that are exploiting natural resources.

The essence of ownership is the sole right to control what is owned and this is a central point in The Theory of Human Rights. The right applies to whatever is owned and therefore includes businesses and premises. A person may select who will work in his/her business or occupy his/her premises and apply any criteria whatever. This is the owner's right but in practise it is unlikely to create the mayhem in society that is feared by modern democracies. If an owner applied unpopular criteria in hiring or renting out premises then he/she would be resented by the community which undoubtedly would be bad for business and could degrade a landlord's reputation. After all, most businesses want to appeal to as many people as they can. In any case, the idea that an owner may not discriminate in hiring or renting originates in social design, not true rights.

The issue of abortion was covered in the previous chapter but The Theory of Human Rights provides a necessary plank for the argument against abortion. It presents fundamental rights as intrinsic to every human being. Once the baby in the womb is established as a human being - the exact point being debatable- the baby possesses those rights.

Another issue is the place of the marriage institution. The right involved is the right of people to join together to manifest anything about themselves that they choose provided the rights of others are not transgressed. They may form associations, clubs, separate enclaves, societies and so on. By that right the heterosexual population has the right to a formal ritual for uniting a man and a woman in a conjugal relationship (marriage). The homosexual population has the same right which is to create a ritual like marriage for formally uniting a homosexual couple.

Homosexuality and transgender phenomena- Heterosexuality is mainstream humanity and necessarily so. It brings new people into the world, replacing those who die and thereby continues the human species. It also follows the obvious design of nature which is male-female coupling. Homosexuality cannot make these claims. Therefore, promotion of homosexuality and biological abnormalities as equal in value and therefore in status to heterosexuality does not conform to those assessments of reality.

If the theory of human rights is accepted as valid, as it should be if no one can point out genuine errors or omissions in its development, then it has the authority of universal truth. Therefore, governmental systems, customs and ideologies that conflict with the theory are correspondingly wrong. Their continued use and practice can only be justified if some people prefer the old way regardless of its inconsistency with true human rights. There is the proviso of course that certain fundamental rights, such as that to personal security and to basic freedom, are inalienable and not negotiable. Nevertheless, the Theory of Human Rights is an indispensable guide to proper governance.

The Theory of Human Rights provides an essential bulwark against governments that give themselves unlimited authority. The fascist governments of the 1930's were an example of this. When Nazi war crimes perpetrators were brought to justice at the Nuremburg trials the prosecutors soon realized that transgressions of German laws were insufficient for fully implementing justice. They had to look to natural law, as they perceived it at the time, to cover the worst crimes. If they had had an accepted theory of fundamental rights their task would have been much easier. If new governments are now set up on a base of true human rights theory the excursion of those governments into abusive totalitarianism will be precluded.

The foregoing theory, in total, provides necessary support for the concept of proper government by explaining its proper birth, mission, authority and accountability. It also provides necessary flesh to its mission of protecting people's rights. A government in action is more than theory, however; it is practice too. Therefore, a concise description of policies and methods that could be expected to go with a proper government follows.

Policies

The foregoing treatises predicate the following policies for a proper government. Generally, the government will operate like a business with its mandate being to fulfill its defined purposes effectively and efficiently. All employees will be expected to fulfill all the responsibilities described to them for their particular job. (This will be covered more completely under "Methods".) The collection of revenues and disbursements of government funds will be done solely by electronic means that provide records of all transactions. (This will be covered more completely under "Methods".) Theft or deliberate misdirection of funds will be sufficient reason for disciplinary action, dismissal or prosecution depending on the gravity of the case.

With every citizen being an equal shareholder in the government employment opportunities in the government must be available to all citizens equally such that only their qualifications for the job are determinants of their getting it (assuming their adequate availability). Job interviewers will not ask the tribe or religion of the person being interviewed. If necessary to ensure impartiality the gender will be hidden. Prejudice in hiring or conduct on the job will be reason for disciplinary action or dismissal.

The judicial system will operate from the meaning of justice being the concept that a person gets what he/she deserves. It will employ punishments that coincide with a public consensus on what standard methods to employ for the different crimes that occur but in no circumstances will the punishment exceed the total pain/harm/damage of the crime after all intangible harm has been accounted for, not only to the victim but to the community at large. Punishments will not be chosen on other bases such as ideological goals or just to set an example.

The national government will require all businesses that extract commodities from the natural environment to purchase the equity of all citizens by direct payment to their accounts via a central bank that automatically distributes the combined input at regular intervals. These transfers will not be taxed. Government may invest in businesses and may start new businesses when they are needed to support general government objectives. It is not the intention of government to actually operate business because operation by private hands has been proven worldwide to be more efficient. From revenues to government through its investments the government may keep a reasonable profit and transfer other funds to approved programs. The money kept as profit is available for emergency needs, cost overruns in approved programs, and for future approved programs. Any remainder in the revenue fund will be distributed to all citizens equally without taxation.

Generally, taxes will be levied on a quid pro quo basis. The tax on a person's earned income will be estimated as a percent owing to the government for its role in providing a safe environment and support for business. The national government will maintain a central bank. Its principle duty will be to authorize the purchase of goods and services using a currency that represents in total the aggregate value of everything in the country that has commercial value. The aggregate value will vary year to year as new things are created while the value of all existing things depreciates. Consequently, the central bank must add or remove currency to suit the net result. Money created may be lent to commercial banks at an interest rate that suits the credit market with the interest revenue going to pay the cost of the central bank and the remainder going to the government as profit. Interest charges by the central bank and by the borrowers from client banks must be taken into account in money supply calculations.

The national government will not favour the creation nor sustenance of political parties but will not ban them. Instead, the government will support an electoral office that will do most of what a political party would do, that is, recruit candidates, train and advise them, and popularize them through standardized presentations for all candidates. The office will also provide a judicious amount of money for election expenses so that every candidate has a fair chance of success. In the legislature, all voting will be by secret ballot but for each member his/her record of voting will be made public prior to the next election.

The government will attempt to divert the input of ideology to the appropriate chartered jurisdiction and away from the national or sub-level government.

Lobbyists will be tolerated but each must register, providing appropriate information that includes contact information, who is paying them and why.

Trade arrangements must accord with the government's plan for economic development, especially in the food production sector.

The national government will take a concerned international view on the protection of endangered animal species, including in the world's oceans. The government's position is that these natural assets are a common heritage of all mankind.

Police forces will enforce the law as passed by the legislature and apprehend offenders without prejudice to their distinctive appearance, gender, tribe, religion, social status and so on. The police will not be employed to implement ideology.

Methods

A proper government will follow the specifications of a well composed constitution document that is intended to treat all the governed fairly. The methods for implementing it must be effective but also respectful of rights. Going forward with the Constitution requires that every person working in the government swear a pledge of loyalty to the Constitution with the understanding that the provisions of this document come first, that is, before directives from seniors in the government. Therefore, directives that seriously violate the Constitution do not have to be obeyed. This requirement applies as well to members of the police and armed forces.

A proper government must, almost by definition, be effective and efficient. To achieve these goals on a full time and ongoing basis the following method will be employed. It requires firstly that the responsibilities of the head of a branch or department of the government are completely and accurately stated. Then he/she must sub-divide the responsibilities into manageable parts and find a person who is capable and willing to accept part of the executive's responsibilities. All the subordinates of the executive must, in turn, sub-divide their responsibilities and find immediate subordinates to accept them. The process should continue as a tree-like structure as the organization takes shape with people filling the positions. When the process is done every position in the organization should carry a list of responsibilities. The theory of this model is that if every person in the organization fulfills his/her responsibilities then the mission of the organization will be accomplished by definition. Ensuring that goals are reached requires that any underperforming employee is coached until performance is corrected. If it is not corrected in the time available then the employee must be replaced. A corollary of this method is that the job security of any person in the organization depends on him/her fulfilling the responsibilities of their position. Seniority and people connections count for little.

The government will make use of the latest technological means for handling money so that all transactions are traceable and qualify for completion by appropriate criteria that ensure that all revenues and disbursements are from/to previously approved business affiliates. Financial audits will be performed often enough to ensure the honesty and correctness of government financial transactions.

In keeping with its primary duty to manage the natural environment the government will divide land for present generations according to entitlements. Each person has an equal entitlement, measured by value, and that of a family is the sum of member's entitlements. They would have a free lease on the entitlement but have to pay rent for any excess. To accommodate the entitlement of future generations the government would hold an adequate supply of worthy land in reserve.

Polygraphs (lie detectors) will be employed where the truth of verbal testimony is vital or where only verbal testimony is available. Therefore, polygraphs will be used when recruiting police officers and some military people. Also, when processing applications for immigration where credible documents are lacking or absent. In all these cases the polygraph can be a useful aid in judging the truth which is what the interviewer is trying to determine.

All police recruits will undergo psychological testing to filter out those with potentially problem personalities that could surface when dealing with the public. Military personnel would receive thorough training in those skills required for military operations, including both spoken and written communication. Computers may be used for individual instruction.

In every part of government service a particular attitude toward problems must prevail. It is that problems must be solved, not tolerated interminably. This is another major divide between democracies today and the ideal of proper government. In the former it is considered sufficient to work against difficult problems, and preferably be seen working against them, but actually solving the problem is not required. In proper government someone in the government will be responsible for solving the problem and failure to do so will put his/her job in jeopardy.

A government that follows the foregoing prescription for proper government can rightfully be called a constitutional republic because the scope and power of government is limited by a written constitution. Most modern democracies are not true republics because governments assume the right to legislate in any area of human activity and to ignore any fundamental rights (defined earlier) that get in the way.

CHAPTER 4

The Ecalpa Constitution Model

The Ecalpa Constitution is a model document that demonstrates how the lessons of the previous chapter could be implemented in a real political constitution for the fictitious country of Ecalpa. It does not exhaust the possibilities for clever construction ideas or wise provisions to better fulfill its intentions of honest, capable and lasting government. In the main, however, it incorporates those features that are new to political constitutions, features that implement true human rights and entitlements and omit those constructions and modes of operation that have created serious or crippling problems for existing democracies. If it is successful it will be copied, possibly improved, by a group that is sincerely trying to break out of the pattern of marginally successful democracies and establish a proper democracy according to sound political theory.

Bringing together the salient features of proper government that are present in the Ecalpa Constitution, these are-

- Protection of all fundamental rights- this is the basic instruction to all police forces and will be incorporated into the philosophy of military forces in regard to their own personnel and an enemy force or civilian population.

- There is no sacrifice of fundamental rights for the sake of a vision for society as a whole. In all its functions and operations, including the taxation system, the rights of all citizens will be respected.

- Implementation of fundamental entitlements- the theory of human rights shows a natural entitlement to proceeds from exploitation of what nature provided. This will be implemented. The theory also shows that a person owns what he/she creates, including while in the employment of others. This changes the basis of compensation for work in the employment of others and it will be implemented.

- The government is owned by the governed, each of whom is an equal shareholder. This has ramifications in how the government addresses and treats the individual person, forbids discrimination in government services that are provided and supports equal opportunity for government employment.

- As owners of the government citizens will decide the purposes of the government (other than foundational purposes) by a formal process of a proposal with cost budget and voting.

The Ecalpa Constitution

Table of Contents

Introduction

This document describes the national government of Ecalpa that is formed through the will of the people to have a central governing organization for certain purposes that are critical to the existence and operation of the country. It is an application of pure reason to the formidable task of managing a large population containing a variety of tribes, languages and religious affiliations. A basic intention is to avoid a tyranny of a particular group over all others in whatever that group manifests. Consequently, the constitution eschews input based on tribal or religious custom and ideology of the social-political, religious or any other kind because these would constitute a tyranny by those who ascribe to the ideology over everyone who does not. In addition, it does not employ the democratic process in a manner that could constitute a tyranny by the majority. Rather, the subject government uses the democratic process for making decisions on what to do with what is owned in common by the citizens because this is the only practical way to make a decision that respects the equal equity of every shareholder. What is owned in common covers two basic things that are described in Part 1C.

The constitution is based on the view that every citizen is equal in the eyes of the government regardless of gender, age, ethnic group, tribe, religion or any distinguishing feature. This applies in all interaction between the government and the people. Furthermore, the government assumes it is dealing with a population of men and women who are capable of assimilating information, reasoning, and making decisions for which they are accountable. Therefore, their vote in any democratic process is taken as compelling on the government. Consequently, every person is recognized as an individual power in the land but a tribe, religious congregation, business group, labour union or the like is not. Such organizations can be an influence on the government, however, in its task of composing suitable regulation.

Since the national government is the creation of the people they own it collectively (reference 3). Therefore, legislation generated by the government is subject to approval by an assembly of the people's representatives. Legislation that is approved may be passed into law by the signature of the president and thereby become enforceable throughout the country. This provision is exclusive, that is, no law produced otherwise in the country is superior and must defer to this Constitution. Neither may any government, organization or person command allegiance that is superior to that for this Constitution.

The constitution is organized in eleven parts which do not necessarily have the same formula for amendment.

An example of item numbering could be 4C2dvi where:

4= Part No.	C= Section No.	2= specification
d= statement		vi= item

The Constitution is the supreme law of the land. Any law, customary practice or a decision of an organ of state or a public official which contravenes this Constitution shall be of no effect. Further, the assumption of state power in any manner other than that provided under the Constitution commands no allegiance or support of the citizens because their allegiance is to this Constitution which protects them.

Part 1: FOUNDATION
Sections

A. Definition of the Country

B. Establishment of a National Government

C. Relationship of Government to Citizen

D. Duties of a Citizen

E. Rights to be Protected by the Government

References to Part 1

Amendment Quotum

A. Definition of the Country

1. The country in concept

It is history now that in past centuries ambitious rulers constructed a single country from the various tribes and ethnic groups that occupied the region now called Ecalpa. It can reasonably be assumed that the present occupiers, of whatever sub-group, are aligned with their history and culture and want the country of Ecalpa to continue. Further, that most, if not all persons, are willing to defend the country against challengers of all kinds. Those who actually are willing to preserve the integrity and functioning of the country can be called citizens.

Implicit in this conceptual definition is the requirement that all individual citizens are identified to the government so the government knows who its supporters are, and who are the qualified recipients of dividends from the government and natural resource companies. The defined country will have a process of authentication and ascription for any person seeking to become a citizen. See section C for details.

2. The country in actuality

The territory of the country is defined as follows.

Map abc and reference maps show the boundary of the country. These boundaries are considered to be borders with neighbours A,B and C.

B. Establishment of a National Government

1. The national government is hereby formed in accordance with the "Theory of Proper Government" (Ref.3, appended). Accordingly, the citizens of Ecalpa recognize the need for a central government to fulfill the following purposes as a minimum.

   a) To neutralize violent forces from an external source that threaten Ecalpa citizens with physical harm, their property with theft or damage, or bring significant damage to the natural environment or otherwise threaten the interests of the citizens.

   b) To neutralize forces from an internal source that threaten Ecalpa citizens with physical harm, their property with theft or damage, or bring significant damage to the natural environment or threaten unjustified insurrection.

   c) To ensure that all people crossing the border into Ecalpa do so with the permission of the people of Ecalpa (through their national government), whether their intended stay is short term, long term or permanent.

d) To preserve, protect and provide access to the natural environment.

e) To manage natural resources for the benefit of present and future generations of people.

2. Each branch of the national government will have one administrative center that will include the office of the chief executive of the branch. The locations will be as close as practical to the population centers of gravity with due consideration for modes of travel. The locations may be in close proximity to comprise a national capital.

3. The government may set up branch offices and other facilities elsewhere with due regard for the right of citizens to job opportunities that are available from its government.

C. Relationship of Government to Citizen

1. Because the government is created by the citizens (in principle) it is owned by them collectively. Consequently, the government is accountable to the citizens.

2. Key positions in the government, specifically those that determine the direction the government takes in fulfilling its duties, as well as on issues of the day, will be staffed by people elected by the citizens. In such elections every citizen has equal status as co-owner and therefore an equal vote.

3. Since every citizen is an equal shareholder then the government may not discriminate against a person based on irrelevant factors when delivering benefits and services. Such factors would include gender, age, tribe, race, ethnic

group, religion, handicap, sexual orientation and political philosophy.

4. Citizenship can be revoked on the order of the responsible government minister when the citizen in question exhibits a continuing refusal to fulfill the duties of a citizen. It will be revoked automatically if the person in question becomes a citizen of another country or takes up permanent residence elsewhere (more than 6 months per year) because a person cannot, it is assumed, fulfill the duties and obligations of a citizen for more than one country at a time. There is also the reason of natural entitlements that assume permanent residence in the country of citizenship. In such a circumstance the person may reinstate his/her citizenship by taking up residence for at least one uninterrupted year but such provision may not be utilized more than once.

5. Any permanent resident of Ecalpa may become a citizen by declaring to the national government his/her readiness to take an oath of citizenship. For legal immigrants a period of three years of uninterrupted residence will be required to demonstrate permanent residency.

D. Duties of a Citizen

1. The continuing existence and security of the country depends on the willingness of the citizen to defend it when called upon. In addition, this willingness is the basis of the contract between the citizen and the government. Therefore, the citizen is obliged to fulfill military service to an extent that is commensurate with the equal duty of all citizens.

2. The duty to support the government includes voting in elections.

3. The citizen is obliged to support internal security forces in their efforts to protect everyone's rights. This includes reporting offences, cooperating with police forces and giving evidence.

4. The citizen is obliged to cooperate with the judicial system by responding on time to summons to court and providing truthful testimony when called upon.

5. The citizen is required to refrain from despoiling the natural environment unnecessarily because every person has an equal claim to it. In a real sense, nature exists for everyone in Ecalpa.

6. There may be other duties specified in other sections.

E. Rights to be Protected by the Government

1. **Fundamental rights**- these are as determined in the paper *The Theory of Human Rights* (Ref.1), appended, and are repeated below.

   a) Natural rights

      i) A person is sovereign of himself/herself.

      ii) A person owns what he/she creates.

      iii) The permanent residents of a country own in common all that nature provided.

      iv) A person or group may, in effect, own animals through an arrangement with the affected community whereby, as a minimum, the owners take responsibility for the animals.

b) Subsidiary rights

   i) Right to personal security and inviolability.

   ii) Right to choose one's beliefs.

   iii) Right to manage one's life.

   iv) Right of ownership over what one creates, whether in service to himself/herself or others.

   v) Right to security of what one owns.

   vi) Right of access to the natural environment, subject to rules on its care and use.

   vii) Entitlement of every permanent resident of a country to an equal portion of available land, measured by value.

   viii) Right of every permanent resident of a country to compensation for natural resources extracted for eventual sale in a market.

   ix) Right to own animals, subject to regulations imposed by the affected community.

2. **Citizens' rights**- these are specific to the relationship of the citizen to governments formed under this constitution and are as follows.

a) The government will enforce natural entitlements 1bvii and 1bviii in the previous specification for citizens but not for permanent residents who are not citizens because they presumably do not support the government.

b) The citizen has the right, as well as the obligation, to vote in every election, plebiscite or referendum submitted to them by the government unless same are directed at a sub-group in which case the right and obligation applies to members of the sub-group.

c) A permanent resident, including all citizens, has the right to move about the country at will without being monitored by government forces unless the person is detained by police or is under official police surveillance.

d) Citizens and other permanent residents may assemble without arms. They may protest, petition, give speeches or recruit followers but have no permission to damage property and will be held to account for such damages. The police may intervene to protect life and limb or property and may intervene if flow of normal traffic is unacceptably obstructed.

e) A person may freely practice his/her religion on premises that he/she has the right to control. Similarly, a group may do so on premises it has the right to control. On public land or buildings the practice of religion may be limited by consensus or may occur freely if there are no observers or if the group has a permit from the government of the jurisdiction. On private premises the practice of religion may be limited by the owner.

In regard to these restrictions on religious practice no religion will have exemption.

f) Government agents must obtain the permission of the occupants to enter their premises, including vehicles, unless they have an order from a court set up under this constitution or have reason to believe that a person within is in serious danger or a fugitive is hiding within. The burden will be on the government agent to show cause.

g) Where police seize a suspect's goods or records they will make a legible record for their use with a copy to the owner. This provision includes communication records.

h) When the government takes over control of man-made improvements on the land the government will compensate the owners at fair market value.

i) The governments set up under this constitution will regulate commercial transactions to ensure that neither party is cheated. Such regulations will include a requirement for truth in advertising.

j) A citizen or non-citizen who has employment in the country has a right to be fairly paid for the value of his/her actual contribution to the business. The work agreement must be in writing and registered with the government. The agreement must include terms and conditions of employment and payment rates broken down into the following components.

– Affiliation- compensation for committing certain hours of the week exclusively to the designated job, maintaining confidentiality, and upholding the company's good name and reputation. It should be paid on a weekly basis regardless of absence from work on excused leave.

- Production- compensation for the job role based on an agreed amount for each unit of production. It would be proportional to the amount of production.

- Responsibility- compensation for taking the responsibility for mistakes and omissions and possibly for quantity and quality of production. It should be based on time on the work premises if this responsibility is not borne when away from the job and on a full time basis if it is.

3. **Contracted rights**- such rights are obtained in contracts endorsed by at least two parties.

a) Any person of sound mind and age eighteen or more may enter into a trade contract which, it is expected, will confer rights on the parties involved. This freedom applies to both genders and is not limited by race, religion, tribe or any distinguishing feature.

b) The national government and sub-governments will provide court and enforcement facilities for the adjudication of breached contracts, including restitution for injured parties.

c) Contracted rights must yield to fundamental rights (defined in #1) at all levels of government unless a party to the contract has joined a chartered principality that requires partial surrender of those rights that may be surrendered under this constitution. See section 10E.

References for Part 1

1. Robert Stephen Higgins, "Theory of a Country", unpublished (2017), appended

2. Robert Stephen Higgins, "Theory of Proper Government", unpublished (2017), appended

3. Robert Stephen Higgins, "The Theory of Human Rights", unpublished (2017), appended

Amendment Quotum

Part 1 amendments must be approved by 67% of the People's Council

Part 2: STRUCTURE of the NATIONAL GOVERNMENT

Sections

A. Three Branches of Government

B. Government Servants

C. Government Buildings and Facilities

D. Government-Citizen Interface

E. Police Organizations

F. Military Organization

References to Part 2

Amendment Quotum

A. Three Branches of the Government

The government is divided into three branches in accordance with three discrete functions of the government. These are: a legislative branch to pass legislation that normally will become law, an executive branch that will direct the activities of government to accomplish the defined purposes of the government, and a judiciary branch that will provide a court system for conducting trials of offenders of the law and prescribing punishment of those convicted. In more detail the functions of the three branches are as follows.

1. The legislative branch, consisting of representatives elected by the citizens, will follow a process of bill origination, study, debate, revision and acceptance by a committee of legislators, followed by review and ratification by the entire body of legislators.

2. The executive branch is structured on a division between the functions of head of state and head of the government. The former will carry the title "President" and the latter "Prime Minister" or other historically accurate name. Their functions are as follows.

   a) The President will represent Ecalpa in regard to its people, government and country as appropriate at home and abroad. In addition, he/she will hold ultimate responsibility for the proper governing of the country.

   b) The Prime Minister will be responsible for the division of responsibilities into areas of operation and for the definition of the responsibilities of the top executive (minister) in each of those areas. He/she will give direction to ministers as necessary to carry out approved programs and to ensure conformance with the constitution as well as to operating policies and procedures.

3. The judicial branch will function as such systems around the world function which is to acquire evidence and sworn testimonies in preparation for trying a person charged with an offence under the law. The branch will provide an adequately staffed court system for carrying out a fair trial without unreasonable delay and keeping records that are retrievable for later review as may be necessary. The court system, through the presiding judge, will pass appropriate sentences for punishment onto convicted criminals.

B. Government Servants

1. Every position in the government, including security forces and executive positions, will have a complete description of all the responsibilities of the position. The incumbent in each position will be required to fulfil all described responsibilities. A deficit in performance must be corrected by the servant's immediate supervisor who will advise and coach as necessary until a correction is successful. If it is not successful in the time available the servant in question must be replaced. This discipline follows from the theory that if all responsibilities are defined and all servants fulfil them consistently the operation of the government will be effective and efficient as required by its owners, the citizens of Ecalpa.

2. Every person to be hired for a government position will be interviewed, possibly tested, and evaluated as to his/her capability to fulfill the responsibilities of the position. Hiring on essentially other grounds, such as family, tribal or religious affiliation will be cause for dismissal of not only the person hired but of the one who did the hiring.

3. Every person who works for the government is required to pledge allegiance to this Constitution and to report any person who seriously deviates from the Constitution in the performance of his/her duties.

4. Because of the stringent requirements and expectations on government servants the pay and other compensation will be sufficiently high to attract the best talents in the land. Furthermore, payments will be reliable and always on time.

5. Performance evaluations will be done for all government servants on a regular basis to detect and discuss how personal performance can be improved.

C. Government Buildings and Facilities

1. The president's office/residence is a symbol of the country and its national government. Therefore, it must be an edifice that, by its architecture and grounds, instills pride in the citizenry. It must be well protected and preserved.

2. The legislative assembly is a symbol of democracy and the power of the people. It must demonstrate outstanding architecture and sensible location. It must provide a good room for the conduct of legislative activities and offices of sufficient size and air conditioned comfort for working.

3. The supreme court is a symbol of the steady implementation of justice in the land. It must demonstrate inspired architecture in a good location and have adjacent offices for carrying out related activities.

4. The government will provide a residence for the Prime Minister. It will not be lacking in size or comfort and will have adequate facilities for entertaining guests.

5. The government will provide living quarters for all people who serve the government on a full time (24-7) basis. This includes some people in diplomatic service and all military service (except part time militia service).

D. Government-Citizen Interface

1. Because each citizen is an equal shareholder the government regards all citizens equally. It therefore may

not discriminate based on gender, age, race, ethnic group, tribe, religious affiliation, nor any such factor. Therefore, when the government dispenses a general benefit (where all are eligible) or a service to citizens, for example a transportation system, then all citizens may access the service equally.

2. In any interaction with a citizen the government will not assume the role of master and the citizen as servant. Rather, the interaction is between individual people, with one or more playing the role of a government servant with certain limited authority while the citizen plays the role of a part owner of an organization that he/she is addressing in the form of a duly authorized representative. Respect must flow both ways.

3. If a citizen is charged by the police or any other regulatory agency the citizen will be assumed innocent until proven otherwise. Other protection is provided to the citizen in the official police procedures for incidents of police-to-citizen interactions. The presumption of innocence will apply in military courts as well.

E. Police Organizations

1. The country will have a national police force that protects the applicable rights from section 1E and enforces all laws enacted by the national government. Further information is given in section 7A and in the following.

   a) Recruitment to the force will be on a country-wide basis without prejudice to race, tribe, religious affiliation or any other irrelevant factor.

b) Candidates will be attached to a polygraph when they affirm knowledge of and commitment to the Constitution and answer questions related to incriminating history.

c) The national police is also intended to be a worthy organization for the capable and honest person wanting to serve his/her country while enjoying financial security. Therefore, wages will be sufficient to attract the best people and will always be paid on time.

2. The country will have a border security force that will protect the borders from unauthorized entry into the country. They will also establish official border crossings where they will process people wanting to visit temporarily or to immigrate. The applicable laws of the country will be enforced. The following statements also apply to this force.

a) Recruitment to the force will be on a country-wide basis without prejudice to race, tribe, religious affiliation or any other irrelevant factor.

b) Candidates will be attached to a polygraph when they affirm knowledge of and commitment to the Constitution and answer questions related to incriminating history.

c) The border security force is also intended to be a worthy organization for the capable and honest person wanting to serve his/her country while enjoying financial security. Therefore, wages will be sufficient to attract capable and motivated people and will always be paid on time.

d) Favouritism in processing prospective immigrants or visitors or the acceptance of bribes will be cause for dismissal.

F. Military Organization

1. The country will have full time army and air forces to protect the country from invasion by external forces and to project the country's power outside Ecalpa when necessary.

   a) A variety of equipment will be accumulated, stored, maintained and operated to cope effectively and efficiently with all credible threats. All purchases will be made to a military specification that is intended to achieve the effectiveness required and otherwise be optimum value for the cost.

   b) Manpower of the forces will be sufficient to deal completely with any external threat. Training will be sufficiently extensive to take a person (male or female) of any educational background and produce a soldier who is as proficient as the best regular army soldier in the world.

   c) When there is a reasonable doubt of the honesty, crime-free history or commitment of a candidate soldier then polygraphs should be used as an aid.

   d) The military organization defends a rights-based government. Accordingly, personnel in the military will uphold and respect fundamental rights at all times, including war situations. Any soldier or officer can be held to account for transgression of the fundamental rights of any person, whether a combatant or not.

References to Part 2

Amendment Quotum

Part 2 amendments must be approved by 67% of the People's Council

Part 3: LEGISLATIVE BRANCH

Sections

A. National Legislature

B. Members of the Legislature

C. Law Making Process

References to Part 3

Amendment Quotum

A. National Legislature

The National Legislature consists of the People's Council, the Council Director's Office, the National Research Center and the Council Security Office. Their set-up and roles are defined in the following.

1. National Council- a legislating body of xyz councilors who have the power to create, modify or rescind laws. Its functions are as follows.

   a) To examine, discuss and debate bills that are introduced to the Council. The purpose is to evaluate the merits of the bill against the real needs of the country and to omit or include ancillary intentions of the bill so as to maximize the opportunity of improving the laws of the land.

   b) The Council must review a formal request from the President to replace the Vice-President or Prime Minister or a bill from the Council to do the same. The request or the bill must be approved by at least a two-thirds majority. The action then takes place at the command of the Electoral Office.

c) The Council must review a bill, if it should arise, to remove the President from office. On approval by at least a two-thirds majority the President must vacate the office on the command of the Electoral Office of the Judicial Branch which confirmed the President in office after his/her election.

2. Council Director's Office- the Council Director is responsible for providing everything the councilors need to fulfill their responsibilities.

a) This office will provide the building, furnishings, utilities, clerical help, communication facilities and security for the People's Council.

b) The Deputy Director will chair the meetings of the Council, will decide the sequence of speakers, introduce the speakers and maintain order in the discussions according to established custom. He/she will also direct security in the Council as necessary with deference to the professional judgment of experienced personnel.

c) The Director's Office does not have the power to change the content of bills in the Council but may recommend editorial changes.

3. National Research Center- this will be provided to enable councilors to find information on matters before them. Up-to-date information in suitable media will be made available at all reasonable hours.

4. Council Security Office- an adequate security force with experienced leadership will provide full time security for personnel and property. The chief of security will report to the Manager of the Council.

5. The country will be divided into xyz constituencies from which candidates will be elected to represent the people in the government. The constituencies will contain approximately the same number of citizens and the boundaries adjusted every ten years if necessary for population changes.

B. Members of the Legislature

Councillors- the xyz councillors will be elected for a four year term from the political constituencies. Each candidate for election must be a citizen and pass a qualifying examination to verify that he/she has sufficient knowledge, honesty, soundness of mind and ability to communicate to carry the responsibilities of the role.

Director of the Council- he/she will be appointed by the President so that the President is assured of consistent and reliable operation of the legislature. The Deputy Director will be appointed by the President on the recommendation of the director.

Staff of the Research Center will be appointed by the head of its administration.

Staff of the Council Security Office will be appointed by the head of the National Police.

Support staff for the legislature will be recruited by the Council Director from any source.

Ministerial positions will be filled from candidates nominated by the Council, the Prime Minister or the President. The nominees need not hold elected office. The Council must approve successful candidates and the Prime Minster will assign roles.

C. Law Making Process

1. Bills introduced to the People's Council can originate from several sources identified in the following. Once the bills are completed as drafts they are evaluated without prejudice to their origin. All draft bills or requests for legislation are submitted to the Council Director's office where they are processed into complete draft bills for presentation to the House.

   a) The president's office- in accordance with the president's overall responsibility for the performance of government his office may submit a draft bill or request for legislation to remedy a problem or make an improvement. The president may also submit a draft bill or request as follow-up to election promises that he made.

   b) The prime minister's office- The prime minister will receive requests from his ministers for legislation that is required for the implementation of programs under their responsibility. The prime minister's office will produce a draft bill based on these requests.

   c) The Council may generate a request for legislation from a committee formed to study an issue that possibly contained a problem. If their recommendations include new legislation or the revision of existing legislation then the prime minister may, at his discretion, have a bill made up to be considered by the Council.

2. Bills introduced to the Council will be processed according to established procedures and in priority set by the Prime Minister. The Prime Minister will assign councilors to committees to study proposed bills and issues at hand and make recommendations.

3. Bills that are passed by a simple majority of the Council will be submitted to the President for endorsement into law. The President may not refuse endorsement but may require correction of an error or may require approval by 60% of the Council. He/she may send the bill to the Constitutional Committee if he/she is not sure it complies with the Constitution and require their clearance before he/she endorses the bill.

4. Bills signed by the President are sent to the Judiciary Branch for inclusion in the Record of Laws.

References for Part 3

Amendment Quotum

Part 3 amendments must be approved by 67% of the People's Council

Part 4: ADMINISTRATIVE BRANCH

Sections

A. Executive Divisions

B. Responsibilities of Executives

C. Primary Interfaces

References to Part 4

Amendment Quotum

A. Executive Divisions

The executive divisions are the President's Office, the Administration Division and the Prime Minister's Office.

1. **President's Office**

   a) Chief executive- the President of Ecalpa

   b) Second executive- the Vice-President of Ecalpa or the Prime Minister

The organizational design and hierarchy of the President's Office and the Prime Minister's Office are the responsibilities of the President and Prime Minister respectively.

The President's Office will have its own security force under the command of the President. It may also be employed to protect designated people in the government and visiting officials of other governments.

2. **Administration Division**

   a) Chief executive- the Vice-President of Ecalpa or Prime Minister

b) Second executives- heads of departments

The Administration Division consists of many departments, the organizational design of which is the responsibility of the President or his delegate. Its purpose is to implement the services provided to the population by the national government. It may also support the efforts of the People's Council.

c) Director of the Council- reports to the Prime Minister on matters before the Council and to the president or his delegate on matters concerning the legislative facility.

3. **The Cabinet**

a) Chief executive- the Prime Minister or his deputy

b) Second executive- Ministers in the National Government

B. Responsibilities of Executives

1. The President of Ecalpa

a) The President has the basic and primary responsibility of ensuring that Ecalpa has a properly functioning national government that remains consistent with the Constitution.

b) The President is responsible for keeping lower levels of government in conformance with the Constitution of Ecalpa in all their legislation and operations.

c) The President is head of state and represents the country of Ecalpa both internally and externally.

d) The President may take an active and even commanding role in foreign affairs but will usually delegate some or all of such matters to the Minister of Foreign Affairs.

e) The President is responsible for reporting annually to the people on the state of the nation.

f) The President makes a second review of bills passed by the Council for conformance with the Constitution and may employ the Constitutional Committee of the Judiciary for a ruling.

2. The Prime Minister

a) The Prime Minister is responsible for composing a list of responsibilities for each of his subordinate ministers.

b) The Prime Minister is responsible for all drafts of bills that originate with himself or his ministers being well composed, complete and presentable to the People's Council. He may enlist the help of the Director's Office in this task.

c) The Prime Minister is responsible for evaluating all bills before the Council such that he can give informed recommendations on their passing or not.

d) The Prime Minister is responsible for assigning people from the Council to committee work and ensuring they adhere to a reasonable schedule.

3. Cabinet Ministers

a) The ministers will be accountable for all items in their list of responsibilities. They must report periodically to the Council on the state of their ministry.

b) Ministers must appear in the Council to answer questions when scheduled to do so. Elected ministers may vote in the Council.

4. Director of the People's Council

   a) The Director is responsible for the effective and efficient operation of all service divisions of the People's Council. These will include the following.

      i) Building services

      ii) Security

      iii) Editorial office

      iv) Standard forms and design of documents and presentations

      v) Utilities

      vi) Supply of consumables

   b) The Director is responsible for the People's Council having everything it needs to perform its legislative function, including a proper venue, furniture, recording devices, secretarial assistance, climate control, lighting, instruction on procedures and so on.

   c) The Director is responsible for the literary composition and presentation of all bills originating outside the Council, including from the President's Office.

5. Deputy Director of the People's Council

   a) The Deputy Director will chair official meetings of the People's Council.

b) The Deputy Director is responsible for scheduling all activities in the Council, including speakers, reporting, debates, and question periods.

c) The Deputy Director is responsible for maintaining order in the Council. He/she may employ security people in doing so.

C. Primary Interfaces

1. President- interfaces directly with his/her staff, the Prime Minister, the head of the Administration Division, the Ministers of Foreign Affairs and Defence and with the Director of the People's Council. In times of war or crisis he/she may interface directly with heads of military branches, including the intelligence group.

   He/she interfaces indirectly with other ministers through the Prime Minister and indirectly with the People's Council through the Director of the Council.

2. Prime Minister- interfaces directly with his/her staff, the President, the Director of the Council and all ministers of the Cabinet.

3. Ministers- they interface directly with their staff, the Prime Minister and indirectly with the President through the Prime Minister (except for #1 above) and with the People's Council through the Prime Minister or the Director/Deputy Director of the Council.

4. Director of The People's Council- interfaces directly with his/her staff, the President, the Prime Minister, the Deputy Director, and Councilors.

5. Deputy Director- interfaces directly with the Director, the Prime Minister and Councilors.

References for Part 4

D. Amendment Quotum

Part 4 may be amended with the approval of 55% of the People's Council.

Part 5: JUDICIAL BRANCH

Sections

A. Design of the Branch

B. Operation of the Courts

C. The Electoral Office

D. Relations with the Citizenry and Employees

References for Part 5

Amendment Quotum

A. Design of the Branch- this will be done by the Chancellor of the Judiciary with professional assistance. The design will be chosen from the world's best working examples and will be added as an appendix to this Part. The design will include the following divisions.

1. **Judicial courts-** for adjudicating cases against civil law and criminal law. Duties of these courts may be divided with the courts of subsidiary governments. Only courts set up under this Constitution are valid.

2. **Supreme Court-** for adjudicating cases of infringement on provisions of the Constitution, for hearing cases of appeal from lower courts, and for cases of claim or suit against the action of the national government.

B. Operation of the courts- will be constrained by the following.

1. All persons charged with an offence will be assumed innocent until proven guilty.

2. Courts will be completely objective without prejudice to chosen beliefs such as religion, superstition, cultism or ideology that cannot be proven to be absolutely true.

3. A person cannot be prosecuted for breaking a law that did not exist at the time of the offence but can be prosecuted for offending a fundamental right (1E1) because such rights always existed.

4. The hierarchy of law is: Constitution/ laws/ regulations.

5. A person will not be required to testify against himself/ herself or family members.

6. Those charged with a criminal offence must have the option of hiring professional counsel and to trial by a twelve person jury of his/her peers. Courts must prove guilt beyond a reasonable doubt.

C. The Electoral Office- will be included in the Judicial Branch. It will have the following character and functions.

1. The Office will organize, notify, prepare candidates and conduct elections-to-office and referenda/plebiscites. The Office will maintain a registry of eligible voters. Voting will be by secret ballot.

2. The Office will interview and test prospective candidates for capabilities needed in the office for which they are running. Disagreements between the candidate and the Office will be settled by an impartial ombudsman for the Branch.

3. The Office will be provided with sufficient security personnel from the National Police to ensure that all

citizens can safely vote and cast ballots are secure before and after counting. Security must ensure that results are completely credible.

4. Disputes involving the activities of the Electoral Office will be settled in the Supreme Court.

5. The Office will confirm selected representatives to office and will order vacation of office on failure to be re-elected. It will also order the vacation of office for any executive whose cancellation of service has been decided by 60% or more of the People's Council for cause

Relations with the Citizenry and Employees

1. Trials will be viewable by the news media and a limited number of citizens. Verdicts and sentences will be publicly announced.

2. Witnesses will be protected from harm as necessary.

3. The privacy of innocent people will be respected.

4. All employees of the courts and the Electoral Office will take an oath of obedience to the Constitution, the Branch regulations and approved procedures.

5. An employee who breaches the trust or propriety of his/her office may be dismissed.

References for Part 5

Amendment Quotum

Part 5 may be amended with the approval of 67% of the People's Council.

Part 6: EXTERNAL SECURITY

Sections

A. Executives

B. Military Organization

C. Intelligence Gathering

D. Military Justice System

References to Part 6

Amendment Quotum

A. Executives

1. The Minister of Defence will be the commander-in-chief of the armed forces. In this capacity he/she will have the following responsibilities.

   a) To translate instructions from the government (normally through the Prime Minister) into explicit directives to the head(s) of the armed forces branches.

   b) To ensure that the actions of the armed forces are consistent with government instructions as to what is accomplished and any specified constraints on how it is accomplished.

   c) To ensure that the actions of the armed forces are consistent with the Constitution, particularly the interrelationship between the government and the military and the respect for the rights of people with whom the military becomes involved, whether military people or not.

d) To appoint the head of the combined forces based on recommendations to him/her.

e) To pass through to appropriate military officers funds allocated to the armed forces by the government.

2. The Chief of Military Staff will cover all branches of the armed forces. He/she will be responsible for the following.

a) Issuing explicit orders based on directives received from the Minister of Defence.

b) Appointing heads of each branch based on recommendations.

c) Ensuring that funds allocated are spent optimally toward the effectiveness and efficiency of the forces.

d) Liaison arrangements between the military structure and the intelligence service.

e) Appointing the head of the Office of Defence Intelligence.

f) Identifying specific missions for the Office of Defence Intelligence.

g) Ensuring that training programs are designed and implemented to achieve training objectives in all branches of the forces.

3. The branch head of each of the forces will have the following basic responsibilities.

a) Ensure that the force is ready in all respects for deployment. This includes equipment, supplies, personnel, training and instructions.

b) Appointment of capable senior officers who are properly motivated.

c) Make complete, accurate and comprehensible reports to higher authority.

d) Ensure that training programs are implemented in an effective and timely manner.

B. Military Organization

1. The commanding officer of each branch must design a military organization for his/her branch. The counsel of the other branch heads must be obtained and the approval of the commander of all branches and the Minister of Defence before the design is implemented. The design should also incorporate the wisdom of other military organizations in the world.

2. The design of the military organization may be placed here as an amendment to Part 6 but will require approval of the People's Council. Alternatively, the organization design may be added as an appendix to Part 6 which requires only the approval of the Minister of Defence.

3. Only present or past members of the military may wear a military uniform or military medals and awards.

4. Forceful action against enemies of Ecalpa must be approved by the Minister of Defence, the Prime Minister and the President. At the soonest opportunity the concurrence of the People's Council, by majority vote, must be sought by the Prime Minister. A declaration of war may be made by the President after concurrence by a vote of 60% or more of the Council.

C. Intelligence Gathering

1. The Office of Defence Intelligence will obtain information on threats, from an external source, to the security of Ecalpa and/or its citizens. The information will be organized and processed to learn the magnitude and sources of the threats and to report same to the government and to the President.

2. Offensive covert actions against perceived enemies in other countries must be approved by the Minister of Defence and the President.

3. The organizational design, staffing, operational methods, approvals and procedures will be secret within the military organization and revealed to government staff only on a need-to-know basis.

D. Military Justice System

1. Because the military system may operate outside of Ecalpa it may have its own justice system. It is also useful inside Ecalpa because military compounds are not readily accessible, because of security precautions, for in-country police forces. Nevertheless certain crimes must be handled by such police forces so that all the protections of an offender, such as presumption of innocence and trial by jury, are provided. Such crimes would be murder, physical assault that cause a permanent disability (lifelong compensation therefore being due) or require the victim to remain in hospital more than 25 hours for treatment, or rape.

2. The military establishment may choose to transfer an offender to the civilian justice system for practical reasons such as shortage of trained staff but are obliged to cooperate with the civilian authority in regard to gathering and storing evidence, securing the prisoner and so on.

3. Under battlefield conditions a military unit may request a mobile court unit from the Judiciary. This would relieve field officers from the duties involved in building prosecution and defence cases, recording proceedings and the distracting responsibility for due process by court. This would apply especially to cases of enemy combatants or civilians committing war crimes.

4. The Chief of Military Staff will design the justice system with the assistance of a committee of the Judicial Branch. That committee will take responsibility for the military justice system having all the design elements necessary to carry out an acceptable implementation of justice. The Minister of Defence must approve the design.

References for Part 6

Amendment Quotum

a) Amendment of Part 6 requires approval by 60% of the People's Council.

b) Revision of appendices requires the approval of the Minister of Defence.

Part 7: INTERNAL SECURITY

Sections

A. National Police Organization

B. Strategic Police Service

References for Part 7

Amendment Quotum

A. National Police Organization

1. The Minister for Internal Security will form a committee for the design of the National Police organization. The committee will include knowledgeable people from the government and also from outside as necessary to recruit the best talent. The committee will study best designs of similar organizations in the world and compose what is best for Ecalpa.

2. The final design will include a Chief of Internal Security. He/she, the Prime Minister and the President will approve the final design, after which it may be implemented.

3. The final design may be recorded in this section as an amendment or as an appendix to Part 7.

4. The National Police will provide subdivisions for specific purposes where deadly weapons are necessary. These subdivisions will work to the requirements of the responsible executives to whom they are assigned. Included are the following.

a) Border Patrol- to patrol the country's borders to catch smugglers and to intercept migrants and advise them to go to official border crossings.

b) Border station security- The Border Patrol will provide security as necessary at border crossings where immigration and custom officials are processing visitors and immigrants.

c) Electoral Office security- whenever and wherever the Electoral Office requires protection from interference, theft, damage to property or security for personnel this force will be available. It will also ensure that voters have clear access to polling stations and safe return from it.

d) National Assembly security- this group will work under the direction of the Director and Deputy Director of the Assembly to ensure a safe place for all who work there.

B. Strategic Police Service

1. The less visible Strategic Police Service will investigate crimes that are less visible and will train specialized groups for such criminal activities as bribery, embezzlement, extortion, human trafficking, organized crime, money laundering, in-country terrorism, distribution of prohibited substances, political conspiracies, computer-based fraud and other secretive criminal activity.

2. Methods used by the service will include surveillance, infiltration, filtering of records, use of informants, and use of contractors who find situations where crime is regularly

committed and assist in getting evidence. Normally, incriminating information will be passed to a regular police force which will apprehend alleged criminals and conduct a usual investigation from then on.

3. This service will be organized by the Minister for Internal Security with the assistance of experienced police personnel from inside and outside the country.

4. The service will make an annual report to the minister on the state of systemic crime in the nation. The Prime Minister and President should also hear this report.

References for Part 7

Amendment Quotum

a) Amendments to Part 7 require the concurrence of 55% of the People's Council.

b) Amendments to an appendix to Part 7 require the approval of the Minister of Internal Security.

Part 8: OTHER PURPOSES of the NATIONAL GOVERNMENT

Sections

A. Prescribed Purposes

B. Determination by Plebiscite

C. Implementation

References to Part 8

Amendment Quotum

A. Prescribed Purposes

The fundamental purposes of the national government, which gave rise to its birth (in principle), are stated in section 1B. These purposes predicate legislation that will manifest them legally.

Seeing a national government in place, with its power and authority, it can reasonably be inferred that it is the only body that can effectively control certain centrifugal forces that threaten people's rights or the ability of the population to function as a collaborative society. The aforementioned purposes include the following and possibly others as they may be seen in the future. They will be implemented by appropriate legislation.

1. Implementation of justice- the national government will provide a system of courts which will try people who have offended the national law. Indeed, this is the purpose of the Judiciary Branch. The national government may also provide a court system for trying civil cases consisting

mostly in breaches of contracts unless such courts are provided by a sub-jurisdiction.

2. Immigration laws and processing of immigrants- the national government will create laws and procedures for the processing of immigration applicants and visitors. The laws will reflect the preferences of most of the population and will not be based on ideology or other ulterior motives.

3. The national government will provide a system of currency and a central bank to facilitate commerce. The central bank will have an account for every citizen into which entitlements will be placed on a regular basis (see 9B).

4. Prevention of the exploitation of people- the national government will undertake the following.

   a) Inspection of food for safe eating and bottled water for safe drinking.

   b) A national standards organization for developing and disseminating safety standards for manufactured and fabricated products.

   c) A national building code to ensure that building structures have sufficient safety and appropriate durability for the purpose.

   d) Regulation on truth in advertising and labeling.

   e) Regulation on investment management by financial institutions to ensure disclosure of relevant factors to investment, proper accounting and transparency, and safe keeping of client's funds.

f) Regulation on insurance companies to ensure that premiums are based on the risk for individual clients.

g) The national government will regulate the telecommunications industry to prevent the exploitation of people through lies and half-truths, eavesdropping, mining of personal information, nuisance solicitations, offensive advertising, and messages designed to generate hate for a particular group of people.

h) Regulation on working conditions, age limits and the like to provide reasonable conditions for paid work activities.

i) Regulations to safeguard people from intrusions into their privacy and right to choose what messages to receive.

5. The national government will control permanent intrusions on the natural environment such as dams, pipelines, electricity transmission lines, windmill farms and so on.

B. Determination by Plebiscite

The people of Ecalpa may utilize the national government for any purpose they choose provided the rights of people are not transgressed and the purposes of government, per Part 1, are not compromised nor the purposes in Section 8A crippled by compromise. The process will occur in the following way.

1. The national government will put forward a proposal to the people who will vote on it in a plebiscite conducted by the Electoral Office. The proposal must show the scope and limits of the planned service and a budget. If money must

be borrowed for fixed assets, then it must be borrowed on a project basis, that is, a definite amount designated for a particular project. The loan must have a definite term and amortization payments which are included in ongoing costs. Ideally, the new service can be paid for from available tax revenue. If a part of the cost must come from a pool of money that is normally distributed to the citizens then the plan must show the expected reduction in regular payments.

2. All citizens are obliged to vote in a national plebiscite.

C. Implementation

1. If a proposal achieves a successful result in a plebiscite it should be added to Section 8B by an amendment. The approved amendment will authorize the government to proceed with implementation.

2. The proposed budget becomes a firm budget and the scope of the actual service provided must be adjusted to it.

References to Part 8

Amendment Quotum

Part 8 may be amended with the approval of 55% of the People's Council.

Part 9: FINANCIAL MANAGEMENT

Sections

A. Financial Management Organization

B. Sources of Revenue

C. Allocating Funds

D. Control of Disbursements

References to Part 9

Amendment Quotum

A. Financial Management Organization

1. The top executive will be the Minister of Finance and he will be responsible for the design and staffing of an organization to receive all money paid to the government and dispense it for approved activities and programs.

2. The design should be informed by similar organizations elsewhere in the world and utilize expertise from inside and outside the government. It must include a transparent accounting system that enables intelligent decisions to be made from study of amounts spent against value received.

3. The final design must be approved by the Council of the People. It should then be added to Part 9 as an appendix to facilitate revisions. Minor revisions must be approved by the Minister of Finance and by the Prime Minister for the Council. Major revisions may be sent to the Council for approval if the Prime Minister decides.

B. Sources of Revenue

1. Taxes- there are several types the government may use.

   a) Income tax- the income of an individual person may be taxed because the person earned the income in an environment and an economic system maintained by the government. The proportion that is claimed by the government for its contribution must be determined by the Minister of Finance based on recommendations from a committee set up for that purpose or by an outside financial management firm. The proportions may vary with type of income or level of income if justifications can be shown. The decided proportions that will be taken as tax on income must be approved by the People's Council. Subsequent changes must also be approved by it. After approval these numbers predicate how much the government will receive from this tax.

   b) Cost recovery taxes- these are determined on a quid pro quo basis for facilities or services that the government provides to citizens or businesses. In most cases a judgment must be made on the division of the cost of a facility or service between the user and the general public. This division will correspond to the relative benefits to each party, recognizing that people who do not use a facility or service still benefit indirectly from those who do use it and by its being available to them or their visitors when required. The general public's portion will be paid from other government funds.

It is reasonable that the government should receive an excess of revenue over cost similar to what a private business would do if they provided the facility/service.

The following examples do not necessarily limit the scope of this source of revenue.

i)   Taxes on vehicle fuels to recover part of the cost (see above) of building and maintaining the system of roads.

ii) Tax on tobacco products to recover the costs to government attributable to people consuming tobacco which would be substantial if the government provided medical care facilities.

iii) Similar to tobacco are alcohol and recreational drugs.

iv) Sales tax to recover the cost to government for maintaining a system of currency.

v)   Tax to pay for access roads and bridges attributable to the operations of individual companies.

vi) vLicensing fees to recover costs for issuing licenses.

vii) Harbour and airport use fees for the security and infrastructure that the government supplies at airports and harbours.

viii) Processing fees for people applying for passports, immigration visas, visitors visas (unless waived to attract visitors), import permits and so on.

2. Return on Investments

a) The national government may invest in all manners of legitimate businesses and financial instruments both at home and abroad, with the intention of earning a positive return on capital that it set aside from government revenues.

b) The scope of the investment program may include providing the genesis of new businesses, especially ones that contribute to the government's strategic objectives: for example, to feed the nation.

3. Assets Recovered from Crime

The government should make every effort to recover funds and assets stolen from the population or the government, either directly or indirectly. The stolen funds and assets should be returned to their rightful owners. If it is impractical to do so, as judged by senior staff, then the recovered funds and value of the assets become available to the government for re-direction. Some may be used to pay for police services and for incentives to police staff, particularly those involved in dangerous situations.

C. Allocating Funds

1. Selected people in the Financial Management Organization (FMO) will have the authority to pay parties that have a right to payment from the government. All payments above the unregulated level- as determined by the Minister of Finance- will be recorded and subject to audit.

2. Government expenses will be paid firstly from tax revenue and then from money recovered from criminal activity. If

these sources are insufficient then the rest may be taken from the national investment account. If money is left over from the first two sources it will be transferred into the investment account.

3. Unused money from the return on investments will be distributed quarterly to the accounts of all citizens in equal amounts from an account in the central bank set up for that purpose.

4. Money may not be borrowed to pay normal operating expenses of the government. Instead, operating expenses must be trimmed as necessary.

5. When the People's Council passes a bill to require all individuals and businesses that are exploiting natural resources to buy out the equity of the citizens the government must implement it. The government will do this by calculating the money due on each unit of commodity extracted and requiring all those responsible to calculate total payment due and deposit it into the same account in the central bank where payments will be recorded and possibly audited. The government will require the central bank to distribute the money to all citizens equally on a monthly basis.

D. Controlling Disbursements

1. All people with whom the government receives or makes payments must have a bank account in a stable, reputable bank that records all transactions. The accounts will be used as follows.

a) All payments to the national government will be done by cheque or electronic funds transfer.

b) All disbursements from the government to citizens will be done electronically and often automatically and a yearly statement issued to record amounts.

c) All destination accounts for government disbursements must have been previously vetted for conformance with terms of an agreement, contract, or legislation.

2. Government accounts will be audited yearly and a report given to the Minister of Finance. Copies will be given to the People's Council and the President. The minister may be required by the Council or the President to explain discrepancies or inconsistencies and to take action.

References to Part 9

Amendment Quotum

a) Part 9 may be amended with the approval of 67& of the People's Council.

b) An appendix to Part 9 may be revised in accordance with preceding section A3.

Part 10: POLITICAL SUB-DIVISIONS

Sections

A. Division of Country into Sub-Jurisdictions

B. Structure of Regional Governments

C. Operation of Regional Governments

D. Municipal Governments

References to Part 10

Amendment Quotum

A. Division of country into regions/provinces/cantons.

1. The country may be divided into regions in the expectation that a regional government will focus more accurately and with more dedication on the distinguishing features of the region. These could be any of: dominant natural features, the most important industry, geographical near-isolation, or an almost universal feeling among the people of a unique identity.

2. The region should be called a province or other suitable political term and brought into being by a bill passed in the People's Council. The bill should name the province, define its boundaries, include the requirements of the national government and direct the setting up of a regional government as soon as practicable.

3. People who want to live under the discipline of a social-political ideology or a religious prescription or any club-like manifestation of humanity may set up an alternative domain. All people who live in such a domain must be

volunteers and must be free to leave. Children must be free to leave on reaching the age of seventeen.

4. People of a region who want to separate from Ecalpa may do so by a process that takes into account the rights and entitlements of every citizen. The process should follow steps a-d.

    a) If a group of people want to initiate the process they must present to the President a petition to do so. The petition must include endorsements representing at least one tenth of the population.

    b) The President must acknowledge the petition and decide whether to reject it or send it to the People's Council for consideration.

    c) If the People's Council decides to proceed with it an order will be issued to the Electoral Office to conduct a referendum on the question. The threshold level at which the referendum will be considered successful will be decided by a simple majority vote in the People's Council. All citizens in the greater jurisdiction(s) affected by the proposal will vote in the referendum.

    d) If the referendum is successful a new country or possibly a confederate state will be constructed. The area of the new country/state will be approximately the same proportion of Ecalpa's area, measured by value, as the proportion of the vote for separation. Initially, there will be a transition zone until it becomes clear how many people who are advised to move actually move. The border should be finalized in a reasonable period of time.

B. Structure of Regional Governments

1. The national government is a ready model for regional government structure but those governments do have the freedom to deviate. Yet, they must conform to the following requirements.

   a) The rights stated in section 1E must be respected by regional government and if necessary legislation passed to protect them.

   b) The regional government must negotiate a split of income tax between the two levels of government because the total proportion taken from an individual is pre-determined (see section 9A).

   c) A tax should be calculated on a quid pro quo basis for each individual subject unless the region has been set up under a charter for an alternative domain (see 1d following) where tax may be designed on other than a quid pro quo basis.

2. An alternative domain must be defined by a charter that specifies the boundaries of the canton (or some other suitable political term), the rights that must be surrendered and to what limits. It should also state important policies, especially for interfacing with other jurisdictions. The form of government must not systemically frustrate the role of the national government in protecting fundamental rights.

C. Operation of Regional Governments

1. Regional governments must comply with and uphold the laws of the land and the stipulations of this Constitution as

it pertains to regional governments. It is on this basis that the national government creates the regional government.

2. Being a creation of the national government, the regional government has no authority to secede in total from Ecalpa, nor to disestablish itself.

3. The regional government must create legislation for the management of land. Per section 1E the land of Ecalpa is owned in common by all the people of Ecalpa (permanent residents whether citizens or not). Therefore, the regional government must do the following.

   a) It must calculate the entitlement of each person in value of land, based on the land that is declared available for people presently living and what land is held in reserve for future generations. Presumably a family would combine their claim to one property, but if a child were to leave on reaching maturity his/her claim would travel with him/her.

   b) A land lease system must be invented that includes terms developed through an effort to learn what the majority of citizens want. This would include such things as length of lease, first option to children if the parents die, and so on.

   c) The rent for the entitled amount would be zero but excess over the entitlement would be subject to rent set by the government.

   d) The rent proceeds would accumulate in the central bank account linked to exploitation of natural resources.

D. Municipal Governments

1. The government structure will be similar to the best proven municipal structures in the world. All members of the legislative body must be elected, including the head of the government.

2. The municipal government is accountable primarily to the superior regional government.

3. The tax power of the government is restricted to a quid pro quo basis. This implies that the government may not redistribute income either overtly or implicitly in its tax laws.

4. The government may rely on the national government to bring water to the municipality from a distance if it is not sufficiently available locally. The national government is responsible for all citizens having access to natural water.

5. As the national government is responsible for the long term preservation of the natural environment the municipal government may claim expenses if it fulfills part of that responsibility within its borders.

6. The municipal government may claim part of the vehicle fuel tax to pay for municipal road infrastructure.

7. The government may participate in shared cost/benefit projects with other jurisdictions.

8. The government may borrow for projects but not for operating expenses.

References for Part 10

Amendment Quotum

a) Part 10 of the Constitution may be amended if more than half of the People's Council approves.

b) Appendices may be revised if the Prime Minister and the President approve. The President may delegate his/her approval.

Part 11: METHODS AND POLICIES

Sections

A. Guiding Principles of the Government

References to Part 11

Amendment Quotum

A. Guiding Principles of the Government

1. The government is determined to fulfill the role laid out for it in the Constitution. Accordingly, it will require all employees of the government, including all military and police personnel, to pledge allegiance to the Constitution in all assigned roles.

2. Because each citizen of Ecalpa is an equal shareholder in the government, it will concern itself with the individual first and the group second, not the other way around.

3. Where applicable, government decision makers will defer to justice with the understanding of justice as the concept that a person gets what he/she deserves and it has a positive or negative sense: reward for meritorious conduct and punishment for offensive conduct.

References for Part 11

Amendment Quotum

Part 10 of the Constitution may be amended if more than 60% of the People's Council approves.

CHAPTER 5

A Possible New Age

From the Old to the New

There have been previous ages of mankind. The ancient Greek poet Hesiod wrote of five ages: the golden age of mankind, the silver age, the age of heroes, the bronze age and the iron age. To those we could reasonably add the industrial age and the technological age that we are now in. Such organization captures only part of the human experience of course. There is the intellectual arena where it could be said that we have had the age of the gods, the age of magic, the Christian era and have recently entered what could possibly be called the secular age. In the political arena there was the age of kings followed by the age of empire: the Greek, Roman, Mongol and British empires. The feudal period was interspersed with empire building and then came the modern era, consisting of government of the people, for the people and by the people. If the theory of chapter 3 and its demonstration in chapter 4 become a norm then a new age will be introduced that could be called the era of proper governance where the term has been defined previously.

The hallmarks of this age will be a low tolerance for nonsense and a high value on justice, not only in the courts but in the business world and in the utilization of nature. There will still be plenty of nonsense because people have an ingrained habit of simply choosing what to believe instead of thoroughly analyzing a situation because it can be serious mental work. In the new era, however, nonsense will not be forced onto people in the regulation of their lives. The countries that will undergo the most reform- if proper government takes hold at all- are theocracies that force people to conform to religious precepts. A proper government will not permit this because its primary purpose is to protect the fundamental rights of every person and these rights include the right to choose what to believe from among the various religions of the world or to choose none. They also include the right to manage one's life as one chooses, including what career path to follow, who to marry, whether or not to have children, or even to choose sexual expression that contradicts one's biological gender. The scope for freedom is bounded only by other people's fundamental rights, government laws, contractual commitments and rules that one has agreed to follow.

Like religious societies countries can be dominated by social-political ideologies that are based in optional beliefs. Generally these beliefs start with a model of the population and apply the morality and values of the authors of the ideology to it. There may be many followers but never the entire population (historically). A proper government would not permit an optional ideology to regulate the jurisdiction unless everyone in the jurisdiction is a volunteer. The reason is the same as for a religion: people have a right to choose from optional beliefs. This right is not acknowledged in modern democracies and is their fundamental fault. Instead, the intellectual forum is dominated by the certain belief that altruistic government is soundly based on indisputable moral principles. It will take a revolution to convince the congregation that morality is chosen, that it is simply another optional belief, and the indisputable principles for which they ache are the principles of true fundamental rights in a world of autonomous human beings.

Cultural mores and customs can constrain people unnecessarily long after the reason behind them has evaporated. A proper government will include a ministry of culture that attempts to improve culture by encouraging the phase out of counterproductive customs and the addition of customs that make life easier, safer and more harmonious. Conceivably, this could range through protective apparel, organization of language, limits on advertising freedoms, polite customs, to the place for charitable organizations in the overall operation of the jurisdiction. A good culture facilitates, is uplifting and supportive, not oppressive.

Proper government will go by a proper definition of justice that will apply to the individual person and not be compromised by a design for society on the whole. The definition that will probably prevail is that justice is the concept that a person gets what he/she deserves. Importantly, it is the individual that is the subject of justice, not the group unless the intention is to render justice to every member of the group based on his/her merits or demerits. Justice can have either a positive or negative sense: reward for meritorious conduct or punishment for offensive conduct. Either one should be commensurate with the value of the former or gravity of the latter and not be contaminated by ulterior motives. This is the guideline that a proper government will follow.

Justice will also be done in the workplace. A worker will be paid for what he/she actually contributes to the revenue of the company rather than being paid on a time basis. Therefore, as stated in the Ecalpa Constitution, a worker will be paid for-

Affiliation

- Compensation for remaining available during specified hours of the week, maintaining employer confidentiality, and upholding the employer's good name and reputation

- An amount per week regardless of absence from work on excused leave

Production

- Compensation per agreement for job role, where the agreement specifies the payment figure for each unit of production created by the worker

- Proportional to the amount of production

Responsibility

- Compensation for being accountable for mistakes and omissions, and possibly for quantity and quality of results

- On the basis of time on the work premises if this responsibility is not borne when at home

- On a full-time basis if the worker bears the responsibility even when at home

Work contracts of this type manifest the right of a person to ownership of what he/she creates while in employment. Those who create more will earn more which is fair. In the population on the whole, wealth will tend to accrue not only to those who have money to invest but to those who create and in proportion to the value of what they create. The net result should be wealth distribution that is more just.

Implementing the right of ownership over what a person creates across a nation will transform the capitalist system into a dual equity system with business owners owning one part of the business- mainly the fixed facilities, special knowledge and business connections- while the employees will own the value of what is created on a daily basis. The business owners will buy out the employees' equity so they can sell the products in the marketplace. This may seem like a less profitable enterprise for the business owners but reductions in orders or losses in the marketplace will be shared with employees through their pay for production and this will assuage the fall in profits.

A career in business will look different in the new era because of the potential to prosper by contributing as much as one can to the business. Those who, for one reason or another, are not inclined to contribute much of value will not prosper because the system will not reward them for nothing and proper government will not require them to do that. A net result, however, will be high efficiency which should have indirect benefit to all by providing more goods and services at a fair price and more sustainable utilization of natural resources.

Another right that will transform society toward justice is the collective ownership by the population of all that nature provided. Its implementation will require that all businesses that exploit nature for valuable commodities from above or below ground must buy out the equity of the collective owners before selling the commodities to others. Since every citizen is an equal shareholder in the collective holding, then each will receive equal payment from every company that is actually exploiting nature. The total result will be a regular payment to every man, woman and child in the country as a return on their equity in its natural resources. It is one of the most meaningful results in the setup of proper government as a contract between citizen and government with government enforcing rights and natural entitlements and the citizen meeting obligations. This raises the interesting possibility that government might withhold the dividend if the citizen fails to meet an obligation, e.g., voting.

With every citizen receiving a regular dividend for his/her equity in what nature provided and receiving fair pay for his/her contribution to a business the welfare state will not be necessary. The taxation system will show this along with the reformed basis for taxation presented in chapter 3. There will still be a place for charity organizations for people suffering misfortune or who cannot earn much from work. There is the possibility, of course, that the population may successfully get the government to undertake a "safety net" program for those left behind in the reward-for-accomplishment economy. Such a program would be subject to the constraints of the taxation system which is not allowed by the Constitution to deliberately re-distribute wealth but which allows the government discretion in spending its earnings.

To summarize the transition from old society to a new society the belief that a common standard of morality and set of common values supply the essential constraints on human behaviour will give way to the notion that morality and values are chosen by each individual person as is his/her right and the restraint on behaviour is respect for each other's rights. The difference will be measured in amount of liberation or in the degree of personal freedom.

Other differences will matter profoundly. Governments will not be permitted to assume rights of ownership over private property, even to implement a non-discrimination policy. Consequently, there will probably be more congealing of identifiable groups in cloistered enclaves than there is now, perhaps even a patch quilt design of different societies. The will of the majority will not apply to any subject area that a legislature chooses but only as a means to decide what to do with what is owned in common. For the population as a whole that is what nature provided and the government itself. What people want will not be the guiding light for government but rather what rights people have because the former generates destructive antagonisms and the latter brings order based on justice. On the whole a person will be free to chart his/her course, subject to other people's rights and laws based on rights, in a similar manner to how they follow their intentions when behind the wheel of a vehicle on the public roads.

Power will be restrained by rights to a much higher degree than now. This will be true in the business and political arenas where the dual equity system will produce just desserts to all players in business and accounting records in government will show where all government payments went and from where all deposits into employees accounts came. With no paper money and only electronic funds transfers all transactions will be traceable.

In the envisioned political firmament three guideposts stand out: honesty, rights and freedom.

Destiny

Looking down the span of time, perhaps a millennium or two into the future, we can ask what government should do for people. Leveling the population in economic terms and blending them together in a herd model is one vision that is very popular in modern democracies, as well as dictatorships, but does not include the most fundamental aspirations of mankind which are justice and opportunity on an individual basis. If a society lacks these qualities it will stagnate and eventually fail. People will not exert themselves or take risks if the reward is clearly not commensurate. Their ambition will die if there are no opportunities. Therefore, a decision must be made. Which path should the world attempt to go down: the present socialist liberal path or the path of a just and free society held in place by proper government? Which would be better for our grandchildren and their grandchildren? It is time for sober reflection on what we want government to be. More of the same or a government that is as good as people can put together and operate?

One thing is clear: the problems of modern democracies will not go away. National debts will continue to rise, to be a burden on future generations; wealth will continue to concentrate to the accounts of incredibly few people, organized gangs will continue to poison populations with addictive drugs, causing more casualties than a war; people will be exploited, their rights ignored, by any organization that seeks power and wealth at any cost. In parts of the world poverty will facilitate the scourges of starvation, disease, exploitation and crime. Yet, this dreary view of human life is not all there is. Everywhere there are valiant souls who try to improve conditions and to deal with the problems in their lives. If government was more effective against the systemic problems there would probably be many who would enthusiastically support it.

There is the world today as it is and contemplation of how to solve its problems but there can also be contemplation of where the world, or more to the point, where humanity should go. Is there a destiny for mankind? Webster's dictionary defines destiny (one meaning) as the indissoluble connections of causes and effects. In the past the causes have been a predilection for superstition, invention of gods to explain natural phenomenon, and more recently, invention of social theories to explain the revolution in life style brought on by the industrial revolution. In the last four centuries, however, reason has emerged as a natural, fundamental force. It has displaced superstition, made great headway against unprovable beliefs in the supernatural, and is bearing down on optional social-political theories that claim too much dominance. The rise of populist parties attests to that. Transcending social theories and politics is the issue of mankind's destiny, at least if one can put aside the battles of today and look into the future. Young people will probably see humanity place its stamp on every walkable part of the solar system with machinery on parts that are not walkable. When an adequate propulsion system is invented unmanned probes will be sent out to neighbouring star systems and when information is received back manned expeditions will set out and the projection of human civilization to other worlds will begin. By that time we had better have our philosophy right. We do not want to export our delusions and hatreds. We need to get rid of them. However we manage our philosophies and politics, it is probably inevitable that mankind will go to other worlds because the tendency of the human mind, as seen especially in the past few centuries, is to expand as far as it can go.

Conclusion

There will be many who evaluate this treatise for its utility in the political and economic arenas, but more than utility is involved. There is the matter of rights. If a utility-minded person two centuries ago had discussed the prospect of freeing the slaves he probably would point out that the economic disruption would be unacceptable and impractical. Yet freedom came because the slaves had a right to be free, as every human being does. The Theory of Human Rights, presented in chapter 3, included the right of ownership of Nature's bounty by all residents concerned (collectively) and the right of the creator of something to ownership of what he/she created. The theory made the case that these rights, being based in natural ownerships, are real. Therefore, a proper political system should implement these rights despite opposition. Their implementation would have such profound effect on society as to replace the welfare state and create a new era that would be most notable for its justice and opportunity. Where the welfare state was concerned with the appearance of society at a distance a properly governed society is concerned with justice for the individual, seen up close and personal.

Was there ever a golden age? The one described by Hesiod was created by the gods. If there is another one it will have to be created by man. Knowing man's vices, however, there will have to be regulation, so there must be government and it will have to be a proper government. This book has laid out the road map. Others may improve upon it or not but in any event the idea must continue.

finis

References

Aldrich, John H. (2011 July) Political Parties In and Out of Legislatures, Oxford Handbook of Political Science

Davis, J.C. (1983) Utopia and the Ideal Society: A Study of English Utopian Writing 1516-1700, Cambridge University Press

Helyer, Paul. (2014) The Money Mafia, Time Day LLC

Jackson, Robert J. And Doreen. (2008) Comparative and World Politics, 5th Canadian edition, Pearson Prentice Hall

Micklethwait, John & Wooldridge, Adrian (2015) The Fourth Revolution: The Global Race to Reinvent the State, Penquin Books

Ryan, Alan. (2016) On Politics: A History of Political Thought, Liveright

The Economist (2014 August 23) The Trouble with Electing Judges, https://www.economist.com/united-states/2014/08/23/the-trouble-with-electing-judges

Fabisiak, Michal, (2017 July 24) How Judges Are Selected Across Europe, Radio Poland http://archiwum.thenews.pl/1/10/Artykul/317562,How-judges-are-selected-across-Europe

Corder, Hugh (2016 March) How Commonwealth Countries Have Forged a New Way to Appoint Judges,

The Conversation, https://theconversation.com/how-commonwealth-countries-have-forged-a-new-way-to-appoint-judges-56090

Ceci, S.J. & Williams, W.M. (1997) Schooling, Intelligence and Income, American Psychologist 52(10), pg 1051-58

Hon. Paul Hellyer & emdash (2012 May 11) The Bank of Canada: The people's bank? http://www.youtube.com/watch?feature=player_embedded&v=p8mlwxBpaTU

International Monetary Fund- for financial data, https://www.imf.org/en/About

Bank of International Settlements- for financial data, https://www.bis.org/about/index.htm

The World Bank- for financial data, https://www.investopedia.com/terms/w/worldbank.asp

Web sites provided information on organizations and data from reports.

The Electoral Commission of the United Kingdom http://www.electoralcommission.org.uk/england

Vision Launch http://www.visionlaunch.com/Pros_and)Cons_of_Political_Parties

Medium Economy http:/www.medium.com/@russroberts/do_the_rich_capture_all_the_gains_from_economic_growth

OpenSecrets.org http:/www.opensecrets.org/fara/registrants

Economics Online http:/www.economicsonline.co.uk/Business_economics/Nationalisation.html

http:/www.britannica.com/topic/liberalism

About the Author

From a humble beginning in a coal mining town on Cape Breton Island Robert Stephen Higgins graduated from the University of Toronto in Mechanical Engineering (1964) and commenced an interesting engineering career. This included several years at the Boeing Airplane Company in Seattle as an Associate Research Engineer on the 747 project before moving to the power industry where he spent most of his career. Power station design work on fossil fired and then nuclear stations carried him to the United States (Arizona), Argentina and South Africa.

Along the way he married Ivanka Vrdoljak and had five children.

Introduction of an employment equity program by his large employer caused him to focus on human rights. In 1999 he took early retirement to pursue the question of what fundamental rights every person has. This culminated in his first book Human Rights, What Are They Really? (Bradich Books, 2008).

Governance for a New Era also takes the engineering approach of completely objective analysis while looking at government in the coming decades.